WINNIPEG
AUG 3 1 2017
PUBLIC LIBRARY

WITHDRAWN

THE KILLER WHALE WHO CHANGED THE WORLD

D1225313

WITHDRAWN

THE KILLER WHALE WHO CHANGED THE WORLD

MARK LEIREN-YOUNG

DAVID SUZUKI INSTITUTE

GREYSTONE BOOKS

Vancouver/Berkeley

For the southern resident orcas

Copyright © 2016 by Mark Leiren-Young

17 18 19 20 21 5 4 3 2 1

All rights reserved. No part of this book may be reproduced,
stored in a retrieval system or transmitted, in any form or by any
means, without the prior written consent of the publisher or a
license from The Canadian Copyright Licensing Agency (Access
Copyright). For a copyright license, visit www.accesscopyright.ca
or call toll free to 1-800-893-5777.

Greystone Books Ltd.
www.greystonebooks.com

David Suzuki Institute
www.davidsuzukiinstitute.org

Cataloguing data available from Library and Archives Canada
ISBN 978-1-77164-351-1 (pbk.)
ISBN 978-1-77164-194-4 (epub)

Editing by Nancy Flight
Copyediting by Shirarose Wilensky
Proofreading by Stephen Ullstrom
Cover design by Peter Cocking and Nayeli Jimenez
Text design by Nayeli Jimenez
Jacket photograph © Jeremy Koreski
Printed and bound in Canada on ancient-forest-friendly paper
by Friesens

We gratefully acknowledge the support of the Canada Council
for the Arts, the British Columbia Arts Council, the Province
of British Columbia through the Book Publishing Tax Credit, and
the Government of Canada for our publishing activities.

Canadä

"And God created great whales."

GENESIS

"Above everything is God, above God is the killer whale."

BILL REID

Inscription on his sculpture *Chief of the Undersea World* at the front entrance
to the Vancouver Aquarium. Translated from the Haida.

CONTENTS

LOOMINGS

"The Killer is never hunted. I never heard what sort
of oil he has. Exception might be taken to the name
bestowed upon this whale, on the ground of its indis-
tinctness. For we are all killers, on land and on sea;
Bonapartes and Sharks included."

HERMAN MELVILLE, *MOBY-DICK; OR, THE WHALE*

July 16, 1964

THIRTEEN KILLER WHALES break through the pristine water off
Saturna Island to take a breath under the morning sun. Their jet-
black dorsal fins slice through the surf off Canada's west coast and
Joe Bauer can't believe what he's seeing.

Two months. The fisherman has waited two months for this
moment, and now, just as he's packing up camp, the day after the
mission has been abandoned, a pod has appeared—and the whales
are swimming toward the shoreline. "Whales!" shouts Bauer.

When Samuel Burich hears his friend, he can't believe it either
and doesn't even glance up as he yells, "Bullshit!" Then he looks out
at the ocean.

Burich has been commissioned to craft an anatomically accurate,
life-sized facsimile of the ocean's apex predator for the Vancouver
Aquarium. The sculpture of the creature known as the fiercest, most
unpredictable killer on the planet will be the aquarium's centerpiece.
Now, after eight weeks of waiting, watching, and dreaming, a killer

whale is in sight. There's only one thing Burich needs to do with the whale that will serve as the inspiration for his art.

Kill it.

Burich takes his place behind an antique muzzle-loaded Norwegian harpoon gun and lines up his target. The bigger whales seem to sense trouble and swim back out to sea. But the smallest one looks Burich right in the eye.

Burich stares back at his prey and gauges the distance. It's no more than ninety feet away. His gun's range is a hundred.

He braces for the recoil from the gunpowder charge and fires. A four-foot-long, two-inch-thick steel bolt flies over the ocean—a six-hundred-foot line of rope holding three bright orange buoys known as "Scotchmen" trails in the sky like a kite tail and...nothing.

The small whale leaps and vanishes under the ocean, as if taunting the would-be whaler. Burich is devastated. The mission is over. He'll never be able to retrieve the harpoon line in time to prepare a second shot before the pod swims away.

Bauer, who is taking photos from the bluff below, has a better view through his camera lens. Burich has harpooned a whale.

The spear pierced the skin just behind the skull and hooked the killer like a giant baitfish the men could use to catch a bigger whale. And if they had another harpoon ready, Burich might take aim at one of the larger killers diving toward their catch.

Their ears still ringing from the blast, Burich and Bauer race toward their boat. Burich has a rifle to finish the job—and for self-defense, in case the other bloodthirsty creatures want vengeance. Everyone knows these are the planet's most dangerous beasts, the only animal besides man that seems to kill for sport, a whale that will rip other whales to shreds.

As Burich and Bauer chase their victim, two larger whales burst through the water. The vicious killers are doing something unthinkable. They are carefully holding the smaller whale aloft. It's unconscious, possibly dead. This isn't an attack; it's a rescue.

What kind of monsters are these?

CHAPTER ONE

THE SEA BEAST

"Most whales, dolphins and porpoises are peaceful creatures. They have to eat to live, but otherwise they harm neither their oceanic neighbours nor man, unless bothered or injured. How different the orca, which seems to be filled with a burning hatred! Nothing that lives or moves in or on the water is safe from its assaults. Its size, power, speed, agility and disposition have made this black monster greatly feared wherever it is known. As the name Orcinus orca implies, it belongs to 'the kingdom of the dead.'"

JOSEPH J. COOK AND WILLIAM L. WISNER, *KILLER WHALE!*

WHEN SAMUEL BURICH fired his harpoon, everyone knew killer whales were monsters. The bad press for the species started with the Old Testament's scariest sermon—Jonah and the whale. In the first century, Roman historian Pliny the Elder described killer whales as "loathsome, pig-eyed assassins," and warned that "a killer whale cannot be properly depicted or described except as an enormous mass of flesh armed with savage teeth."

In 1758, Carolus Linnaeus, the Swedish naturalist who developed taxonomy, dubbed the creatures *Orcinus orca* in his *Systema Naturae*. The origin of the name depends on whether you believe the root comes from *Orcus* (Rome's god of death or the underworld) or *ork* (from the French term *orque*, which was used to describe sea monsters long before it became the name of the villains in *The Lord of the Rings*). Whichever version you prefer, the Latin translates as "of or belonging to the kingdom of the dead," "bringer of death," or "devil whale."

In 1874, American naturalist Captain Charles Scammon warned that "in whatever quarter of the world [killer whales] are found, they seem always intent upon seeking something to destroy or devour."

The Haida people of British Columbia dubbed killer whales *skana*, which translates as "killer demon—supernatural power." Alaska's Aleut called them *polossatik*—"the feared one." First Nations opinions about killer whales varied, probably based on which whales they encountered, but whether they viewed the creatures as potentially dangerous spirits (as the Haida did) or reincarnations of their ancestors (like the Nuu-chah-nulth), the First Nations in North America respected them as intelligent beings who ruled the ocean just as humans ruled the land.

The German term *Mörderwal* translates as "whale-murderer." Basque fishermen called the creature *ballena asesina*—"assassin whale," which may be the origin of the name killer whale. Both names were inspired by the orca's penchant for hunting and feasting on other whales. All the names in every language conveyed the same warning—these creatures were deadly.

On Captain Robert F. Scott's final Antarctic expedition, in 1912, his men twice found themselves surrounded by killer whales and were convinced they were doomed. Scott's photographer, Herbert Ponting, was on an ice floe with a team of "Eskimo dogs" when a group of whales began circling. He could see their tall triangular black fins and hear their breath through their blowholes—a sound he knew meant danger. For a photographer in love with the natural world, the scene must have been magical—until the attack.

The snow under Ponting's feet began shaking, rocking, and cracking. The booming sound of the creatures ramming the ice floe beneath Ponting and his dog team filled the air. "Whale after whale rose under the ice, setting it rocking fiercely," wrote Scott. "One after another their huge hideous heads shot vertically into the air through the cracks which they had made. As they reared them to a height of 6 or 8 feet it was possible to see their tawny head markings, their small glistening eyes, and their terrible array of teeth—by far the largest and most terrifying in the world."

As the whales set their small glistening eyes on Ponting, he knew it was all over. But after surveying the man and his dogs, the whales vanished beneath the surface and swam off to look for their standard fare, probably seals.

The whales' ingenious, methodical approach to hunting haunted Scott. "Of course, we have known well that killer whales continually skirt the edge of the floes and that they would undoubtedly snap up anyone who was unfortunate enough to fall into the water; but the facts that they could display such deliberate cunning, that they were able to break ice of such thickness (at least 2 ½ feet), and that they could act in unison, were a revelation to us." It was a revelation he shared with the world.

Whales of all types became especially infamous courtesy of American author and whaler Herman Melville. His novel *Moby-Dick; or, The Whale* was released in 1851 to tepid and sometimes savage reviews and less than titanic sales. During Melville's lifetime, *Moby-Dick* sold only 3,200 copies. It was the least successful of his six novels. But in the 1920s, thirty years after Melville's death, *Moby-Dick* became a pop culture phenomenon, an icon and a synonym for whales and monsters after America's silver screen heartthrob John Barrymore starred as a heroic Ahab in the 1926 silent movie *The Sea Beast*. The movie was such a hit that Barrymore revisited the role in a talkie version four years later that kept Melville's name, *Moby Dick*.

Since the 1920s, *Moby-Dick* has been adapted and reinvented for every medium and almost every genre, making a splash on stage, radio, and screen. An epic exploration of obsession and madness, *Moby-Dick* is also a horror story about a savage, unpredictable, unstoppable force of nature. Courtesy of all the adaptations—and there are hundreds, ranging from comic books to sci-fi space operas—*Moby-Dick* did for whales what *Jaws* did for sharks almost a century later.

At the same time that Barrymore was battling the great white whale on-screen, American author Zane Grey wrote about the terror of seeing a killer whale up close. "The fact that my hands shook attested to the knowledge that I had acquired of peril on the sea. Even the veteran whale-hunters are afraid of orca." Best known today as a prolific author of Western pulp fiction, Grey wrote more than a dozen books on fishing and warned his readers that "orca kill for the sake of killing. No doubt the Creator created them, the same as the sharks, to preserve a balance in the species of the Seven Seas—to teach all the larger fish and dolphin, seals, porpoises, that the price of life was eternal vigilance." Grey also cautioned that "orca are the most ferocious and terrible of all the wolves of the sea. They are equally dangerous to man."

The word "whale" was almost always synonymous with monster and interchangeable with giant. Many scientists say the killer isn't technically a whale—it's the largest member of the dolphin family (Delphinidae); pilot whales are the second largest—but the distinction isn't that clear cut. Some experts on cetaceans (whales, dolphins, and porpoises) flip the equation and don't just group killers and pilots with the rest of the species but wonder if the porpoise should actually qualify as a small whale.

IN 1963, JUST before the Vancouver Aquarium's expedition, a book entitled *Killer Whale!* presented the most up-to-date information on the creature Burich and Bauer were hired to hunt. The introduction by Dr. Ross F. Nigrelli, pathologist at the New York Aquarium, warns readers that "the fiercest, most terrifying animal in all the world lives in the sea, not on land. Lions, tigers and great bears are considered savage animals, but many times more powerful and far more vicious than any of these is the killer whale."

Authors Joseph J. Cook and William L. Wisner explain that "from the beginning of time the killer whale has been feared wherever man has depended upon the ocean for food. To the Eskimo, the orca was the wolf of the sea because of its habit of hunting in packs. To the Pacific Northwest Indian, it was the fierce and fearless hunter of the open waters."

The authors offer a collection of terrifying tales about ornery orcas, describing an attack in the Antarctic where several boats were pursued by "a pack of killer whales." The writers report that "the men were able to reach the edge of a nearby ice floe, abandon their craft, and flee to safety on foot. There probably have been many instances where men were not so fortunate. No doubt seal hunters, Eskimos and others traveling alone on the ice have been captured by orcas with no witnesses to tell of their fate."

Moving to the other side of the world, they share the account of "an enraged bull orca" ramming and shattering a twenty-five-foot fishing boat off the coast of South Africa before devouring four fishermen.

The book concludes with a chapter titled "A Living Nightmare" that begins on the ominous note, "This is the true story of five fishermen…" According to this "true story," five men harpooned what they thought was a shark near Long Island, New York, but discovered they'd caught something far more terrifying. The hunter was so scared he dropped his end of the harpoon. "For the first time he saw the animal's evil eyes, the large mouth, the telltale curving patch of white behind the eyes. All at once he knew that a dreaded killer whale was within touching distance!" Not surprisingly, the fishermen survived to tell the tale.

U.S. Navy diving manuals warned that if their fearless warriors found themselves confronted by a killer whale, it was time to get out of the water to avoid being attacked by "a ruthless and ferocious beast." Naval officers stationed in the Antarctic were advised that killers "will attack human beings at every opportunity."

Killer whales weren't just considered dangerous but also useless. In an age when whales were judged by how easy it was to render them into oil, or grind them into pet food and fertilizer, killer whales were a problem even if they weren't killing humans. Whether killer whales are officially considered whales might be interesting to taxonomy buffs, but to fishermen all that mattered was that orcas aren't built like other whales, which made them unappealing to catch. They have less blubber and almost no oil. They also have teeth instead of versatile and valuable baleen. Whales that eat plankton—baleens— have a sophisticated strainer system made of pliable keratin (like human hair and finger nails). That strainer—the baleen, or "whale-bone"—was used like preindustrial plastic to make corsets, buggy whips, and umbrellas.

The Japanese ate killer whales, but the Japanese ate pretty much anything they could find in the ocean. No one in North America developed a yen for killer whales. So fishermen were not impressed by creatures that devoured the same food we did. But that's what rifles were for. Fishermen around the world regularly took shots at the pests North Americans nicknamed blackfish, thrashers, and sea devils.

In 1956, the government of Iceland asked a U.S. naval crew stationed at its NATO base to cull the killer whale population in order to save their precious herring. *Time*, the era's dominant newsmagazine, reported on the mission to slaughter the "savage sea cannibals," which were described as "up to 30 ft. long and with teeth like bayonets."

The unnamed *Time* correspondent wrote that

> this year the largest packs of killer whales in living memory ter-
> rorized the seas off Iceland. They destroyed thousands of dollars
> worth of fishing tackle, forced dozens of Icelanders out of work for
> lack of gear. Last week the Icelandic government appealed to the
> U.S., which has thousands of men stationed at a lonely NATO air-
> base on the subarctic island. Seventy-nine bored G.I.s responded
> with enthusiasm. Armed with rifles and machine guns, one posse
> of Americans climbed into four small boats, put to sea and in one
> morning wiped out a pack of 100 killers. A newsman watched
> an even bigger skirmish off Grindavik and related: "First, the

killers were rounded up into a tight formation with concentrated machine-gun fire, then moved out again, one by one, for the final blast which would kill them. Other whales helped the troops, for as one was wounded, the others would set upon it and tear it to pieces with their jagged teeth. The sea was red with blood. The scene of destruction was terrible. I have never seen anything like it."

But before the readers could get the mistaken impression that anything untoward had happened in this war against whales, the article concluded on a cheery note: "It was all very tough on the whales," reported the newsman, "but very good for American-Icelandic relations."

THE FIRST TIME a savage sea cannibal was captured by humans was in 1961. A group from the world's first major commercial aquarium—Marineland of the Pacific—caught a killer whale in California.

Marineland was created in 1938, when movie producers set up a tank outside St. Augustine, Florida, to shoot undersea adventure movies. After capturing a bottlenose dolphin to headline their films, the owners were shocked when an estimated twenty thousand visitors arrived to meet the star. People were more excited to see the dolphins offscreen than on, so instead of shooting movies, Marine Studios decided to charge admission and the idea of a commercial "oceanarium" was born. The accidental tourist trap became Marineland of Florida, complete with the Marineland Motel, Sandpiper Snackbar, and Moby Dick Lounge. And they still managed to make a few movies, including *Creature from the Black Lagoon*.

In 1954, the idea of an aquarium with big stars went Hollywood with the launch of a second location, Marineland of the Pacific, in Los Angeles. After several failed attempts, the L.A. branch captured its first whale in 1957, when the director of collections, Frank Brocato, and his right-hand fisherman and godson, Frank "Boots" Calandrino, collected a pilot whale. They equipped their thirty-seven-foot gill-netter (the *Geronimo*) with a cowboy contraption consisting of a net, a lasso, and a platform attached to the bow that allowed them to rope their catch.

On February 27, 1957, they tracked a small pilot whale just off Santa Catalina Island, in California. After dodging their snare for nearly six hours—and taking several runs at the boat—the twelve-foot female was caught, positioned on her back on an inflatable raft, and towed to shore. California's children were invited to name the prize exhibit, and the world's first captive pilot whale was dubbed Bubbles. Hollywood's biggest star was born—and so was the model for future marine parks.

The Franks soon captured another pilot to serve as an understudy for the role of Bubbles, thus establishing the tradition (followed by SeaWorld with Shamu) that captive whales are immortal. The first Bubbles choked to death on a rubber ring less than two years after being placed on display.

But pilots were just whales; killer whales were monsters.

No one tried to capture a killer until November 17, 1961, when a lone whale was spotted in California's Newport Harbor. Based on the size and shape of the dorsal fin, the capture crew from Marineland was certain that the killer was female.

The next morning, determined to land the ultimate catch, the two Franks and their crew arrived at the harbor on the *Geronimo*. After several hours of chasing the killer, the crew members realized their lasso wouldn't work and switched to a 1,200-foot-long, 75-foot-deep nylon net. They easily scooped up the whale, but it tore through the mesh almost immediately. After quickly repairing and reinforcing the net, they decided to try again.

An estimated eight thousand people standing on the shore and curious onlookers from roughly fifty nearby boats watched the capture. But not everyone was rooting for the whalers. Americans have always been fans of outlaws on the run, and the audience on the beach cheered whenever the whale dodged its would-be captors and when one of the hunters fell into the water.

After more than eight hours of high-stakes hide-and-seek, the hunters once again netted the whale. This time, their exhausted captive, whom they'd nicknamed Wanda, wasn't going anywhere. The men maneuvered Wanda onto an inflatable raft, as they'd done with Bubbles 1 and 2, and after reaching the shore, they transferred her into a tank on a flatbed truck and drove to Marineland.

Wanda's stay at Marineland didn't last long. According to the official report on the whale, which was referred to as the Newport Specimen:

> Upon being placed into the 100 by 50 by 19-foot oval fish tank at approximately 10:00 PM, the whale initially struck her snout a glancing blow on one of the walls. She then commenced to swim slowly around the confines of the tank, her behavior being similar to that of newly-introduced smaller delphinids. The following morning, the whale was observed holding a newly-killed ocean sunfish in her mouth. This fish was not consumed, however, and during the remainder of the day many attempts were made to induce feeding. Marineland divers attached lines to bonita, and "worried" the killer whale with these as she slowly encircled the enclosure. The animal made several attempts to bite the food and it was at this time that the worn condition of her teeth was first observed. At 8:30 AM on 20 November, the whale became violent and after encircling the tank at great speed and striking her body on several occasions, she finally swam into a flume way, convulsed and expired.

According to the Marineland report, the dead whale weighed just under twenty thousand pounds and was more than seventeen feet long. This seems unlikely, since that would make Wanda the heaviest female orca ever reported—but she was clearly a big whale.

That same morning, pathologists from the Los Angeles County Livestock Department performed a necropsy and determined that Wanda had died of acute gastroenteritis and pneumonia. They also found signs of advanced atherosclerosis and concluded that the stress of the capture and confinement probably contributed to her death. Their report also noted that Wanda's brain weighed almost ten pounds and was very highly developed.

Brocato's recollection of Wanda's demise was more dramatic. "She went crazy," he told reporters. "She started swimming at high speed around the tank, striking her body repeatedly." After less than forty-eight hours, the world's first captive killer whale was dead. But catching a killer whale no longer seemed impossible. The Franks knew they could net another one, and this time they'd find a healthy orca, ideally a juvenile—a whale that could grow up in captivity, a whale they could train to do tricks.

On their first attempt at killer whale hunting, they almost landed a baby. The Franks spotted a calf, roped it, and were ready to reel in their catch when the other members of the pod turned to face them and lined up side by side in what the hunters believed was a military-style attack formation. Rather than risk being charged by an orca army, they set their captive free.

The next time they were ready. They had the gear to catch a whale—and the weapons to protect themselves. They outfitted the *Geronimo* for a trip up the Pacific and arrived off the coast of Vancouver in the summer of 1962. Brocato still had his sights set on a juvenile, but just in case an angry mother or killer whale army attacked, he'd packed a "high powered cannon." Local experts, including Vancouver Aquarium director Dr. Murray Newman, were convinced the whale hunters from Hollywood were risking their lives.

Brocato and Calandrino picked Point Roberts, Washington—a small fishing community just on the U.S. side of the border, roughly fifteen nautical miles away from Saturna Island—as their ideal hunting grounds. The whales might not recognize the imaginary line in the water indicating the international boundary, but Canadian officials would, so the Americans were going to catch a killer on their side of the border to avoid becoming entangled in any political nets.

On September 16, after two months of searching for their prey, the whalers spotted what they believed was a female killer chasing a porpoise. Brocato told Calandrino to watch the porpoise and treat it like bait. The porpoise saw the boat and decided to treat it like an escape route. As the whales focused on the porpoise, Calandrino easily roped his killer—just like he'd caught dozens of dolphins.

But the whale cut underneath the boat, wrapped the 250-foot line around the propeller and then surfaced 200 feet away. "As it emitted shrill shrieks a bull orca rose alongside it—both rushed *The Geronimo*, striking it with their flanks." At least that was how the hunters reported the incident. Whether the whales struck the boat or whether they were chasing the porpoise and the waves rocked the boat and spooked the men, the result was the same. Fearing for his life, Brocato took out his .357 Magnum rifle and pumped ten bullets into the female and one into the male. Moments later, the waters off Point Roberts were red with blood. The dead female killer was floating beside them; the male was gone. The great expedition was over. And the killer whale's reputation as an unpredictable beast, ready and able to destroy anything in its domain, was not only intact but enhanced. The men who caught pilot whales told the world that the killer whales had almost killed them.

The *Geronimo* hauled the female's corpse back to the American port town of Bellingham, where they weighed and measured their catch, which was reported as twenty-three feet long and more than 35,000 pounds (an extreme size estimate that also seems slightly fishy). Brocato kept the sharp teeth as souvenirs. The whale's remains became dog food. The most experienced whale wranglers on the planet were finished chasing killers. They were far too dangerous to capture, and they were clearly impossible to exhibit.

CHAPTER TWO

SAVE THE WHALE

"More than any other denizen of the deep, *Orcinus orca* inspires an emotional response ranging from pure hatred (seamen react to them with the same intensity that shepherds react to cougars) to an unwitting thrill of admiration. In either case no one familiar with the killer whale's savage potential has ever viewed that enormous tower of a dorsal fin, a triangle often six black, evil feet in height, without a tremor in the nether regions of their stomach."

JACK SCOTT, *VANCOUVER SUN*, JUNE 4, 1964

THE SMALL KILLER whale being held aloft in the water off Saturna isn't breathing, but the two larger whales holding it on the surface, waiting for a puff from their pod-mate's blowhole, aren't prepared to surrender. For killer whales, breathing is not an automatic act. If an orca is not conscious, it won't inhale, and it needs to be on the surface to breathe. A killer can hold its breath underwater for about fifteen minutes—long enough to escape almost any attempt by a human to harass it—but an unconscious whale won't live long. And if this whale regains its senses underwater and gasps for air, it may choke and drown before it can reach the surface. As shock sets in and consciousness fades, Burich's victim is drowning. It is about five years old. That means one of the whales attempting to save it is probably its panicked mother or grandmother. The two larger whales consider their injured pod-mate. Is it already dead?

That doesn't matter.

A mother orca in mourning may hold her dead calf above water for days and transport it for hundreds of miles.

The whales off Saturna know their companion isn't dead. Killer whales can see about as well as humans. Anyone who has watched a killer and thought it was looking back at them from the water, or through the glass walls of an aquarium tank, was probably right. Killer whales see well enough to not just identify other creatures but to identify depictions of other creatures in paintings or photos. They can also recognize themselves in mirrors—a test used by scientists to determine self-awareness and intelligence.

But vision isn't the most useful sense when you're diving a hundred meters in murky water. Killer whales listen, using a sense called echolocation, which works like sonar technology. By emitting sound waves and tracking the echoes as they bounce off their targets, these whales can find and "see" anything in the water. As each of these two whales transmits a signal from the front of its head—the melon— they are able to sense the injured whale's heart pounding, to listen to their baby choke as water seeps into its lungs.

Orcas can hear each other's calls from more than ten miles away. Their senses are so acute that they can dive to the bottom of a pool to locate and retrieve an object half the size of a wedding ring. There's a blind Marvel comics hero—Daredevil—whose hearing is enhanced like this, which makes him dangerous enough to defeat armies of ninjas. Orcas basically have the same superpower. They don't just "see" objects; it's possible they can echolocate what's inside of them. There's anecdotal evidence to suggest they can detect whether a female from our species is pregnant before the expectant mother can. So these whales know that their pod-mate's organs are still functioning and that they won't be for much longer. Orcas will work together to support and transport their injured mates for weeks at the risk of their own health.

People who have spent a lot of time around these whales suspect that they also have a sixth sense or, at the very least, an uncanny sense of timing. Ever since Burich and Bauer and the other men in their original hunting party arrived with their weapons, the whales have steered clear of their usual fishing grounds—a route they've probably been following for thousands of years. Maybe it's a coincidence, maybe the salmon were somewhere else. And maybe it's a coincidence that the killer whales only returned this morning, after the plan to harpoon them had been aborted, after the gun was supposed to be gone.

Veteran killer whale watchers and longtime researchers all have stories about the ones that got away. They'll tell you about the orcas that waited until the moment the cameras were no longer pointed at them—or the moment after the film ran out or the battery died—before doing something spectacular. Is it too much of a stretch to wonder if they can sense friend or foe? Some longtime whale watchers are convinced that orcas will perform when they have the chance to endear themselves to humans who are working to save them. Says Erich Hoyt, author of *Orca: The Whale Called Killer*: "Fanatic whale watchers—I've heard them talk—suggest that the friendlies, 'the crowd pleasers,' know their fate rests on humans and that they are on their best behavior with us, putting on one last show as it were before the big curtain, extinction, falls."

Killer whales have also helped humans hunt. In North America and Australia, there are stories of orcas herding fish—and even other whales—to make it easier for fishermen to catch them. In the late nineteenth and early twentieth centuries, orcas near Eden, Australia, would drive humpback whales into an area known as Twofold Bay in exchange for their favorite pieces of meat—the tongue and the lips. This working relationship where the killer whales worked as whale killers for more than a hundred years was referred to by local fishermen as "the law of the tongue."

According to the Eden Killer Whale Museum, "In the early years of Eden whaling in the 1840s there were reportedly around 50 killers spread through 3 main pods. All three pods cooperated together. One pod stationed far out to sea would drive whales in towards the coast, another pod would attack the whale and another pod would be stationed ahead of the whale in case it broke loose." The whale believed to be the leader was a twenty-two-foot, thirteen-thousand-pound killer the whalers named Old Tom. After a humpback had been trapped, Tom would alert the whalers by slapping his tail and repeatedly breaching (jumping out of the water and landing with a splash) to summon the humans to finish off the kill. There were also stories of fishermen falling into the shark-infested waters when their boats were swamped by a humpback and Tom and other orcas warding the sharks off and saving their partners' lives.

In 1923, when a local whaler refused to share his catch and injured Tom in a tug of war that damaged his teeth, most of the pod stopped herding the humpbacks, proving that this wasn't a natural behavior. It was a job, and if the orcas weren't being paid, they weren't showing up for work. But Tom continued to herd larger whales for his taste of tongue. When Tom died in 1930—as a result of the teeth he lost—the people of Eden built their whale museum to honor their longtime partner and display his bones. The Australians of Eden had worked with the orcas for almost a hundred years. The indigenous people of the area, the Koori, are believed to have worked in harmony with the whales for ten thousand years. And anyone who has ever seen a killer whale in captivity knows they can be trained to do practically anything in the water. Killer whales know how to work with humans—and save them—but humans have rarely been inclined to help the killers.

The whales off Saturna knew what humans usually did when they came close in their boats. The humans shot them. But as Burich and Bauer approach, the orcas can't move quickly or far—even if it means risking being harpooned like their pod-mate. They won't let their baby drown.

IN THE EARLY 1970S, Michael Bigg was working as a marine mammal research scientist for Canada's Department of Fisheries, and part of his job was to assess the killer whale population now that orcas were being captured and displayed by marine parks. Fishermen and killer whale "collectors" believed there were thousands, perhaps tens of thousands, of wild whales roaming the Pacific coast.

The initial plan was to tag the orcas, but after talking with Vancouver Aquarium curator Murray Newman, Bigg settled on a more radical idea—simultaneous observations. Over the course of a weekend, volunteers located along the coast would spot and count the killer whales. Bigg sent a questionnaire to fifteen thousand people who lived and worked on the water and asked them to report all the whales they saw on July 26, 1971. Only 549 whales were spotted by volunteer scouts between California and Alaska.

That first census shocked everyone. It didn't seem possible that there were only a few hundred orcas in the region. Then Bigg adopted an even more rigorous—and controversial—approach. In 1973, he and Ian MacAskie—his colleague from Canada's Pacific Biological Station in Nanaimo—were studying whales in the Johnstone Strait when they realized they could tell the individuals apart by the nicks, scratches, and marks on their dorsal fins and the shape of each whale's "saddle patch"—a unique pattern located behind the dorsal fin. Researchers in Africa were identifying individual mammals based on their features, so why not attempt the same approach with killer whales?

Bigg and his partners soon identified all the local pods, designating every group with a letter of the alphabet and numbering each individual whale. The first killer they saw was number one, the second was number two, and so on. The term "pod" is said to have originated from the fact that whales stay close together like the proverbial peas in a pod—and Bigg proved these pods really did stick together.

The idea that every killer whale could be identified on sight was initially dismissed and even ridiculed by other researchers. Not only did photo identification strike other scientists as impossible; no one believed that there were so few orcas off the coast of Washington and British Columbia. The American government was skeptical of Bigg's methods—and his math—and hired its own expert—zoologist Kenneth Balcomb—to determine whether there were more orcas in the U.S. Balcomb, who fondly refers to Bigg as "the crazy Canadian," conducted his own population survey in 1976. Not only did he confirm Bigg's findings, but after launching a whale museum in Friday Harbor on San Juan Island, he began giving all the numbered whales catchy names to raise money for his research and conservation efforts. He wanted to convince people to adopt their own orcas, and it was much easier to convince kids to raid their piggy banks to support Ruffles, Granny, or Princess Angeline than J1, J2, or J17. After the museum had been launched, Balcomb became executive director of the Center for Whale Research in Washington, which doubles as his home. Balcomb has conducted an annual population survey ever since his first count and devoted his life to studying the whales found in the Juan de Fuca Strait, Strait of Georgia, and Puget Sound— an area that was renamed the Salish Sea in 2009 to honor the area's origins and future.

THE ORCA'S FIERCE reputation was well earned.

What Burich and Bauer didn't know, what no one knew, was something else Bigg would discover—that there are multiple types of killer whales, which are so distinct that it is likely that, if they survive long enough, they will one day be considered different species. The different kinds of killer whales—known as ecotypes—don't look exactly the same, and although they are capable of breeding with each other, and have mated when forced together in marine parks, there is no evidence that they have bred with each other in the wild in more than 700,000 years. The mammal-eating orcas that Bigg dubbed transients are as different from the fish-eating whales he called residents as lions are from house cats. Not only do residents and transients have different feeding and hunting habits, but they also have different languages, rules, and rituals. When the two types of whales meet in the wild, the transients tend to steer clear of the residents.

Thanks to aquariums where orcas serve time as star attractions, and movies like *Free Willy*, loveable, chatty resident whales with their close-knit families and seafood diet have captured the global imagination and become the default image not just for orcas but for every whale from belugas to blues. Resident killer whales travel and hunt in close-knit family groups, constantly communicate, and feed on specific types of fish, determined by the part of the world they live in. Studies of dead residents have revealed that their diets are so specialized that when they're living in the wild, they will almost never deviate from it, even if the alternative is starvation. On the west coast of North America there are two groups of residents— the northerns, who roam between southeast Alaska and southern Vancouver Island, and the southerns, who live along the rest of Vancouver Island, including the waters near Saturna. These whales travel all the way down to California.

The orcas who earned killer whales their reputations as monsters were the transients, which scientists now refer to as Bigg's whales. Bigg's whales are less social, less chatty, and less picky about their food. These whales are larger, with sharper dorsal fins. They hunt in packs like wolves—the mammal they have often been compared with by anyone who has seen them hunt.

Humans watching killer whales over the years were convinced that these whales enjoy hunting, since they'll catch a favorite menu item, like a seal, and flip it into the air to kill it. They've also been known to allow their prey to escape before catching it again. These are probably older whales training their children, but regardless of their reasons, the methods earned killer whales a reputation for methodically tracking their prey and also for tormenting it—as if they're playing with their food. After stalking seals and sea lions and punting them into the air until they're dead, they peel the skin off their prey and discard it as if they're snacking on bananas. And their prey includes much larger whales—like minkes, grays, and humpbacks. They are also known to eat other animals that have wandered into or near the water—including birds and moose.

Old Tom and his clan were Australian mammal eaters. When the orcas take down another whale, it's a savage kill, the stuff of nightmares, even for seasoned whalers. This isn't legend; it's reality. Orcas are the ocean's apex predator. There may be no reason for humans to be afraid of transient killer whales—since they rarely attack anything they're not planning to eat—but to any creature that's part of their diet, they are the ultimate black and white horror movie, the destroyer of worlds, death. And since they eat the largest animals on earth, why wouldn't these unstoppable killing machines feast on human flesh?

There are a few theories about why orcas don't attack humans in the wild, but they generally come down to the idea that orcas are fussy eaters and only tend to sample what their mothers teach them is safe. Since humans would never have qualified as a reliable food source, our species was never sampled.

So why wouldn't they mistake us for food if we fell into the water?

Because they don't rely on their sight.

A shark will take a bite of a surfer and then spit it out because, apparently, we're not as tasty as fish and seals. But orcas use echolocation to lock in on their prey. If a human disguised himself as a sea lion, the whale would know that the idiot in the sea lion suit isn't part of a balanced breakfast.

Another possible explanation is that, unlike our species, orcas would never harm another creature they consider intelligent. Even though Bigg's whales eat other whales and don't mix with residents, the mammal-eating orcas don't harm their pescatarian, pacifist cousins.

Because of Bigg's work, scientists and whale watchers now know almost every orca in the Salish Sea on sight. His research led to the southern residents being placed on the endangered species list in Canada in 2001 and in the U.S. in 2005. Today, the southern residents are considered one of the most endangered populations of any species on the planet.

In 2015, the U.S. National Marine Fisheries Service declared the southern resident killer whales one of the eight most endangered marine populations in America, and they are the only officially endangered orca population in the world. At the start of spring 2016, after a year that saw the biggest baby boom since the 1970s, there were only eighty-three southern residents in the Salish Sea. But in 1964, the belief was that there were too many killer whales, they were ferocious, and, at best, they were a pest that should be eradicated.

The young whale drowning off the coast of Saturna was a southern resident, which meant the only item on its menu was Chinook salmon.

IN 1964, IT was the salmon diet that had earned killer whales their designation as public enemy number one. A half dozen years earlier, there may have been enough salmon in British Columbia for whales, but there weren't enough to satisfy humans. Fishermen blamed the killer whales, which were swimming beyond their usual hunting grounds in search of sustenance. Industry leaders demanded that the government step in to solve the whale problem.

Proposals from government officials included arming the coast guard with explosive bullets, bazookas, dynamite, depth charges, and mortars. One plan called for boats to herd the killers into shallow waters so that the air force could bomb the pods. One Canadian fisheries officer suggested using a baited line to entice whales to come close enough to harpoon. He was certain that if the harpoon failed to finish off the beast, the other members of the pod would do the job, saying, "There would seem little doubt that the cannibalistic traits of the rest of the shoal, if left alone, would soon put the finishing touches on him." The fishermen believed that the whales were like sharks and that blood—even from their own kind—would ignite a feeding frenzy.

Finally, the Department of Fisheries settled on a more civilized solution than explosives. In June 1961, a fifty-caliber machine gun was mounted on the Vancouver Island side of Seymour Narrows to kill the whales. Seymour Narrows is roughly 140 miles away from Saturna.

The gun was never fired, but not because anyone protested. It was a dry, hot summer, and there were fears a stray bullet might spark a forest fire. Also, once the gun was mounted, the killers steered clear of the area, just as they stayed away from Saturna after the aquarium's hunters arrived. In 1962, the salmon stocks returned and the fishermen assumed their competitors had already been culled.

The morning of July 16, 1964, the killer whales off the coast of Saturna were using their acute acoustic senses to track salmon. From April to October each year, the whales swim more than seventy-five miles a day and can travel at up to twenty miles per hour as they stalk Chinook, which regularly cozy up close to the shores of Saturna.

On a good day, an adult killer whale eats up to three hundred pounds of salmon.

On a bad day, there are no salmon and the whales don't eat.

On a very bad day, a whale gets hit by a harpoon.

CHAPTER THREE

CANADA'S CAPTAIN AHAB

"Dr. Newman combines the best qualities of Louis
Pasteur and P.T. Barnum. He is a unique public servant
in that he has the complete respect and recognition
of his professional colleagues all over North America
and at the same time has managed to appeal to the
public fancy."

JACK WASSERMAN, *VANCOUVER SUN*, 1963

THE VANCOUVER AQUARIUM was expanding, and Murray Newman wanted a star attraction. Marineland's director had warned
Newman about their catastrophic expedition, so he knew that
killer whales were too dangerous to capture. But Newman's dream
was to feature local marine life in his aquarium, and he considered
the killer whale not just the most impressive aquatic specimen in his
part of the world but "the most magnificent of all living creatures."

On a tour of Europe in 1960, Newman had visited the British Natural
History Museum and was enchanted by its life-sized models—
elephants, a great white shark, and, best of all, a hall of whales, which
included both the skeleton and a replica of a blue whale. Newman wanted his own whale, but unlike the statues in London, he
wanted his model to be a perfect, anatomically accurate replica of
the most feared predator on the planet. This would be scientifically

significant—and it would scare the hell out of little kids. What more could any curator want from an exhibit?

Born in Chicago in 1924, Newman was a self-described "Depression boy." His father had a prestigious publishing job and loved to hunt and fish as a hobby. Then the stock market crashed, and fishing and hunting became a way to feed the family.

"Dad loved trout for breakfast," recalled Newman. "Dad also traded trout with a farmer in exchange for fruit and vegetables." Ever the academic, Newman noted that his father's favorite trout weren't really trout. "They called them eastern brook trout, but they were really char." While Dad angled for breakfast, young Murray lay on the ground watching the fish, studying them, and realized they were fighting. He founded his first aquarium while he was still in elementary school, when he bought a fishbowl from the dime store and regularly spent his allowance on the specimens they kept in the back room. He eventually saved enough money to buy his own tank and learned to care for the few fancy fish he could afford.

After a year at the University of Chicago as a science undergrad, Newman was drafted and joined the navy. One of his first postings was at the Battle of Bougainville in the Solomon Islands. His fondest memory? The tropical fish.

When his stint was over, he completed his degree, then earned a master's in zoology from the University of California, Berkeley. His thesis focused on the behavior of trout—real trout, not the kind his dad had caught. Newman studied the same thing that had fascinated him when he watched his father fish—the way the tiny creatures fought for dominance. He was lured to Canada by fish stories about all of the unique types of trout in British Columbia waters.

Murray and his wife, Kathy, moved to Vancouver, where Newman was awarded the first ever H.R. MacMillan Fellowship in fisheries to help fund his PhD studies at the University of British Columbia. Newman's life changed again when he met his scholarship's patron— H.R. MacMillan. The Canadian lumber baron liked company on his 137-foot converted minesweeper, the *Marijean*. Sometimes he'd take friends—the most powerful men in the province—and catch fish for sport. Sometimes he'd take scientists and catch specimens. Sometimes he'd take both. Newman became MacMillan's go-to naturalist for the next dozen years. MacMillan became Newman's friend and patron, and Newman soon found himself on a first-name basis with the province's powerbrokers.

In 1955, Newman was appointed head of the Vancouver Public Aquarium. It was more of a concept than an institution, but it came with $300,000 in funding commitments from various levels of government. Newman became the first employee of Canada's first ever public aquarium, and it was his job to create... something.

Although Newman's UBC mentors were keen on their student's candidacy, some board members wanted a flashier figure to spearhead the city's new tourist attraction. Already balding at thirty-one, with a slow Midwestern drawl, Newman looked and sounded like a lab nerd—an ichthyologist, not an impresario. But despite his scientific demeanor, Newman was an explorer at heart—always happy to jump into new adventures, preferably when he was in his diving gear, ideally with his wife, Kathy, beside him.

THE AQUARIUM OPENED on June 15, 1956. Admission for adults was twenty-five cents. In the first two days more than 10,000 visitors showed up. By the end of the first year, 342,870 people had passed through the turnstiles. Since the population of Vancouver was only 344,833, Newman celebrated the aquarium's first anniversary with a press release joking that "if you are one of those 1,963 unlucky Vancouverites who did not get around to see the fish in 1957, perhaps you will be able to make it in 1958." He also raised adult admission by a dime.

In 1963, Vancouver city council held a plebiscite to determine whether residents were prepared to pay $250,000 to expand the aquarium. The provincial and federal governments committed to matching the city's contribution. Newspaper columnist Jack Wasserman, the voice of Vancouver, warned that if the aquarium didn't expand, it wouldn't be big enough to contain Newman's ambitions, and the province couldn't afford to let their curator go. "If we lose Murray Newman it will be a tragedy of the first magnitude. Even greater than if we lost the Premier." Newman got his funding. It was time to play Ahab.

"I felt that a lot of the aquatic wildlife was savagely treated and the public should really know more about all of these different kinds of animals. So in planning an expansion I thought, wouldn't it be marvelous if we could sort of symbolize the waters of British Columbia by having a perfect model of a killer whale." Newman wanted a proper sculptor to craft this model. And to make sure the model wasn't just attractive but also accurate, he was determined to kill a whale and then measure it in the water, while it maintained its size and shape. This level of concern for precision was positively cutting edge for the era.

The media was fascinated by the idea of an expedition to track "the marine world's public enemy number one." And in 1964, there was nothing controversial about hunting a killer whale, or pretty much anything else.

A few years earlier, Newman had made headlines when the aquarium caught and killed one of B.C.'s last basking sharks as the model for a similar sculpture. The second-largest fish in the world after the whale shark (real whales are mammals), basking sharks (*Cetorhinus maximus*) grow to forty feet in length, weigh up to ten thousand pounds, have huge mouths with tiny teeth, and pretty much all they do is bask. According to fossil records, they've been preying on plankton for about 30 million years. Most sharks are in perpetual motion, but basking sharks live like middle-aged tourists at an all-inclusive resort—they float in the water, waiting for food to show up. Their dream diet is krill (small crustaceans). The shark's huge open mouth may look like a death trap, but the only way it would hurt a fly is if the fly flew in with dinner.

They are, however, extremely lethal to gill nets (and vice versa), and there were enough sharks basking in the mid-twentieth century that they used to be seen traveling in groups of up to a hundred off the Pacific coast. In other parts of the world, basking sharks were hunted—and rendered—like whales. The fish have oversized livers— up to a quarter of their considerable body weight—which means they're rich in oil. Their skin can be used as leather, their cartilage is sold as medicine, and their remains made fine fish meal. But in 1948, B.C. fishermen lobbied the provincial government to place a bounty on the sharks. A year later, basking sharks were declared "destructive pests" and received the same government-sanctioned death warrant as black bears, seals, and sea lions. It was the job of Canada's fisheries officers to kill these creatures on sight.

The Department of Fisheries turned one of their boats into a killing machine, equipping it with a retractable, triangular steel spike. When sharks were spotted, the *Comox Post* would race to the fishermen's rescue and lower the blade at their bow to save the endangered gill nets by filleting the giant fish. The device spiked more than forty basking sharks in its first month of operation. The *Victoria Daily News* declared on June 22, 1955, that "since no commercial use has been found for the shark, their presence in a salmon school is a fisherman's nightmare." They were also considered a nightmare for the tourist industry. If their submersible skewer wasn't handy, the *Post* followed the same protocol as other large vessels and intentionally rammed the sharks head on—also an effective method of murdering them. Meanwhile, Sunday fishermen happily harpooned the sharks. Some thrill-seekers used them as water skiing ramps and, quite literally, jumped the sharks.

Wildlife was just another limitless Canadian resource, like minerals and trees. The day Newman's appointment as aquarium boss was announced in the *Province*, an ad on the same page featured a sketch of an adorable whale spouting water. The whale was the logo for "100% organic blue whale compost and soil conditioner." Acme Peat Products promised that their whale meal—available "at all garden supply stores"—was "ideal for all phases of gardening and fine green lawns."

Yes, Canadians loved whales—as fertilizer.

Newman asked the Department of Fisheries to approve his plan. The officials didn't just offer their blessing but steered Newman toward someone who could shoot the whale and a scientist who could choose the best spot to set up the harpoon.

The whale expert was one of the men who'd inspired Newman to move to British Columbia—Ian McTaggart-Cowan. Now the head of UBC's Zoology Department—and Canada's first celebrity scientist (his CBC TV show *Fur and Feathers* launched in 1955 and set the table for Dr. David Suzuki's long-running environmentally themed series *The Nature of Things*)—McTaggart-Cowan suggested the aquarium set up camp on Saturna. There was a spot on the island—East Point— where the water was so deep and the whales were able to swim so close to shore that McTaggart-Cowan hoped to build a research facility there.

For the previous four years, June Fletcher, wife of East Point's assistant lighthouse keeper, Pete Fletcher, had kept a detailed record of how many whales, seals, and sea lions she saw each day. According to her records, it was rare for a summer day to go by without a pod approaching the shore, and some of those pods numbered fifty or more.

The aquarium's board put $3000 toward the expedition, and a Vancouver charity offered another $1,000 to the cause. When the project was announced, the media was captivated by the idea of a whale hunt. "The killer whale is more abundant in B.C. waters than anywhere else—it is really a spectacular animal," Newman told reporters before launching his sea safari. "He deserves to be called king of the beasts more than the lion. He could swallow an African lion whole. The public just isn't aware of the magnificence of this animal. We want to emphasize and dramatize the whale by making it the primary exhibit in the foyer."

Newman surprised everyone, especially himself, with his talent for showmanship. According to many people who worked with him, Newman's greatest skill was making everyone feel not just needed but essential. Friends, colleagues, and coworkers—and the labels tended to be interchangeable—all claimed that Newman had honed helplessness to an art form. He never simply asked people to work for him; he convinced them there was no way his scheme could succeed without them. If they didn't come on board with his latest venture, it was utterly and completely doomed. Everyone Newman recruited—whether teenaged volunteers or titans of industry—received a variation of the same pitch:

"I can't do this without you."

NEWMAN ASSEMBLED HIS crew of whalers as if he were selecting master criminals in an *Oceans 11*–style caper movie. He needed a harpooner, an artist, a scientist, and someone to share their story with the world.

Killing a whale is easy—just aim the gun and shoot. Using a harpoon would allow the whale to be killed without doing serious damage to the body or the organs, but it would be challenging. Fortunately, the Department of Fisheries knew the perfect man for the job—veteran fisherman Ronald Sparrow. A respected member of the Musqueam nation, Sparrow knew how to harpoon a whale, and most importantly, he had his own harpoon.

Sparrow had installed an ancient Norwegian gun on his own gill-netter to shoot the killer whales that were chasing his catch. The weapon was a natural whale repellent; the moment it was mounted on Sparrow's boat, the whales vanished. That was good news for Sparrow, but perhaps someone should have taken it as a sign that it might not be the ideal weapon for landing a whale.

Newman found his sculptor by asking the head of Vancouver's Emily Carr Art School to recommend someone who could make an accurate and beautiful model of a killer whale. The answer was thirty-eight-year-old Samuel Burich. Burich had specialized in stone carving at Saint Martin's School of Art in London and was now teaching sculpting at the Vancouver school of art. Not only was he a respected sculptor, he was also a fisherman and marine engineer.

This combination of skills made him the perfect man for the mission, especially since the plan called for him to study the shape of the dead whale and take precise measurements while it was still in the sheltered bay off East Point.

Burich was so intrigued by the offer that he quickly crafted a small sculpture of a killer whale, which he presented to Newman as proof that he was the only man for the job. The most enthusiastic member of the crew, Burich also offered to serve as Sparrow's "co-gunner." He was hired for $300 a month (only $100 less than Newman's original salary for running the aquarium), plus a $500 completion bonus, to craft a whale out of fiberglass and plaster.

Newman's most impressive catch, however, was Dr. Patrick Lucey McGeer. Since Newman was the aquarium's chief fundraiser, his curatorial skills were less important than his political skills, so his choice for a lead scientist was ideal on every front. A world-renowned neuroscientist, the thirty-seven-year-old McGeer had recently been elected a member of the B.C. legislature, representing one of the province's wealthiest communities—an electoral district adjacent to the one where the aquarium was located.

McGeer had grown up in the spotlight. His father was a provincial court judge, his mother was one of the city's only female media stars, and his uncle Gerald Grattan McGeer was arguably B.C.'s most popular politician—a two-term mayor of Vancouver who was also elected to the provincial and federal legislatures.

A scientist and an athlete, McGeer also found himself in the spotlight as a basketball star, leading his university team in scoring to beat the visiting Harlem Globetrotters and representing Canada in the Olympics.

McGeer met his wife, Edith, when they were both doing research at Princeton. After moving to Vancouver to work together at UBC, they began turning their lab into one of the world's most respected neurological research facilities, where they were assembling a huge collection of human brains.

Newman and McGeer first met at a school fundraising dinner. Newman joked that "he [McGeer]was famous and I could read. I said he should really be working on whales. I was beginning to think about this idea of somehow capturing a killer whale and I discussed this with him a little bit and he was hooked."

According to McGeer, Newman was an expert with the hook. "Murray has this marvelous technique of engaging people with something terribly important and then pretending that he's helpless and he can't do it unless you participate. Nobody else I've ever met has this particular skill, but that's how he built the aquarium from nothing. Murray could have gone a long way in politics."

McGeer didn't know much about whales—he'd never even seen one—but he loved the idea of getting his hands—and scalpel—on what promised to be one of the biggest brains in the world. "It was known that dolphins had very large brains and these were sort of like super dolphins," says McGeer. Since this was the height of the Cold War, dolphins weren't just studied; they were being trained by Americans and Russians as potential underwater spies. "I thought if we're going to kill a killer whale, then I'd better get a look at the brain and compare it with the brains of other species."

McGeer was too busy to spend time on Saturna—he had smaller brains to deal with as a politician—but he was touted in all the media coverage. His involvement gave the endeavor an air of gravitas, and other specialists lined up for their piece of orca pie. This was the era of slice-and-dice science—the way to study an animal was to catch, kill, and dissect it. Dr. Gordon Pike, a marine biologist, called dibs on most of the internal organs. Researchers at Vancouver General Hospital wanted the heart and lungs.

Because the hunt was expected to be historic—or at the very least, a great way to capture headlines—members of the media accompanied the team.

Jack Long, a documentary maker for the National Film Board of Canada, was initially on hand to record the historic mission. After Long left the island, *Vancouver Sun* newspaper columnist Jack Scott arrived to chronicle what he described as "the most obsessive whale hunt since Moby Dick." Scott filed a series of special reports on the adventure he dubbed "Murray's Operation Killer Whale."

Vince Penfold, the aquarium's assistant curator, was brought to Saturna as a lookout.

The final members of the crew were the five men serving on the sixty-five-foot coast guard vessel the *Chilco Post*. It was their job to finish off the specimen once Sparrow shot it. Scott explained:

> The plan is this: On the far side of the cliff, beyond *Chilco Post's* view, one of the lookouts will race to the high ground of the lighthouse when the action begins. He will wave a yellow rainslicker. This will be the signal for *Chilco Post* to get into the act. It will run at full speed out through angry waters to the Boiling Reef, around the headland and engage the harpooned whale in combat, following its flight by means of the enormous marker buoys attached to the end of the harpoon's line. When the stricken whale surfaces for air, as, of course it must, the crew of *Chilco Post*, braced at the gunwales will pump a hail of rifle bullets into it.

Then Scott warned of the possible consequences. "No one can say for sure how a killer whale will react if the harpoon does not strike a vital spot and, moreover, there's every likelihood that the other bulls in the pack, or 'pod,' as it's properly known will attack the ship itself, as they have been known to do in the past... Since a bull killer whale runs to 25 feet in length, and has a mouthful of teeth and a disposition that can only be described as perfectly dreadful, the possibilities are downright chilling."

Scott was trying to sell newspapers by amping up the drama, but he'd captured the zeitgeist. The Vancouver Aquarium was hunting a monster, and these hunters were risking their lives.

CHAPTER FOUR

A LIVING NIGHTMARE

"Since the whale in question is the strongest, blood-thirstiest, most unpredictable creature in the seven seas, the party could get rough. We're after *Orcinus Orca*, better known as the killer whale, the only creature other than dear old Homo Sapiens, which kills for the sheer lust of killing."

JACK SCOTT, *VANCOUVER SUN*, JUNE 2, 1964

I F YOU WANT to harpoon a killer whale from the safety of the shore, there is almost no better place on the planet than the northeast tip of Saturna Island, known as East Point. For as long as anyone can remember, orcas have gathered year round off Canada's southernmost Gulf Island, not far from the edge of the imaginary line in the Pacific Ocean that has marked the Canada-U.S. border since 1872.

In 1964, most of the hundred or so inhabitants of this small hilly island lived on the other side, roughly fifteen miles away, near the ferry terminal at Lyall Harbour. The only connection between East Point and the rest of Saturna was a rugged dirt road. Almost no one lived here except the two lighthouse keepers and their families and the past lighthouse keeper and his wife, who'd recently built themselves a small retirement home.

Beyond the cliff, just before the notorious Boiling Reef, which was the reason for the lighthouse, there was a thirty-seven-fathom drop.

In addition to being a hazard to boaters, the reef is a resting area for the roaring Steller (or northern) sea lions, which can grow more than ten feet long and weigh more than 2,500 pounds. Steller babies—and the seals that share their resting spot—are a favorite food of transient killer whales.

The lighthouse—really more of a light tower—with the houses nearby, was surrounded by lush green grass that looked like perfect grazing territory for the island's wild goats. In the spring of 1964, *Sun* writer Jack Scott said that the grass was blanketed with flaming orange California poppies. He described the whaler's campground as "so theatrical in appearance...as looking like a bad set for an improbable movie."

Saturna was "discovered"—as white folks used to say—in 1791, when a legendary Spanish schooner, the *Santa Saturnina* (believed to be the first European vessel constructed in North America), was exploring and charting the Gulf Islands. In 1869, the first British settler, Peter Frazier, set up a homestead, paying the Crown one pound per acre. The Salish knew the island as Tekteksen, which means "long nose"—a reference to the shape of East Point.

On May 20, the aquarium's intrepid team arrived at the long nose in boats and floatplanes. The men were starting to get their bearings when Vince Penfold spotted a pod of killer whales arriving to greet them. It was 6 AM, and it looked like their adventure might be over before breakfast.

This wasn't a big surprise; the hunt was expected to take less than a week. The whalers raced to the bluff, but the whales were gone before Sparrow's gun could be mounted. Although they never got to take their shot, everyone was thrilled. The whales were here.

Pete Fletcher knew the best place to set the harpoon—on the sandstone platform he and June called "the water sample rock." Every day, one of them stepped onto the stone at the edge of the water and dipped a cedar pole with a thermometer and collection bottle attached into the ocean to check temperature and salinity. Samples were sent to the Department of Fisheries, where scientists hoped to learn more about the habits of the salmon stocks that frequented these waters. While the Fletchers collected their samples, they'd often see killer whales surfacing, sometimes almost too close for comfort.

Sparrow and his crew covered the rock with a thick wooden plank and attached the harpoon gun. The recoil from a few early test rounds confirmed that it needed to be secured more carefully. The men collected large stones to weigh down the platform, and then anchored it with a series of chains. The harpoon had the same effect as it had on Sparrow's boat. No whales appeared. During the four previous summers, there had never been a week without a whale sighting. The aquarium had a chance at landing their whale a few hours after arriving, but the hours became days, then weeks.

While everyone was waiting to catch their specimen, the captain of the *Chilco Post* used a hydrophone to collect the strange sounds of the killers that weren't venturing close enough to be shot. The coast guard was experimenting with audio recordings in the hope that playing the apex predator's cries would frighten the sea lions away from valuable salmon.

One afternoon, the *Post* pulled close enough to the camp to share the recordings over a loudspeaker. Everyone was startled by the symmetry and rhythm of the squeaks and squeals. There were patterns that sounded like calls and responses, an almost musical structure that seemed less like random noise than language. Could these creatures be communicating with each other? Perhaps that first whale the men had hoped to harpoon had spread the word about the island's dangerous new visitors.

While they waited for their prey, Sparrow trained Burich to load and fire the harpoon. The two practiced by shooting at a raft towed by the *Post*, but they missed their mark more often than they hit it. Finally, a pod of whales appeared. Burich raced to the harpoon, picked his victim, lined up the shot, fired, and watched as the steel spike and nylon tail whistled over the killer's back.

The would-be model responded with a leap and a dive. Then the pod swam off, toward a part of the ocean where they wouldn't be disturbed. When Canada's fisheries minister, James Sinclair, arrived to survey the operation and watched the whalers practice shooting, he left the island convinced they'd never hook a whale.

On June 2, Scott's column in the *Sun* described the scene: "Our intrepid leader here is Dr. Murray A. Newman. It frightens me to think what will happen to Murray if the hunt fails. I see him as an old, old geezer, roaming the oceans of the world, cursing and shaking his gnarled fist at the empty waves. The way things are going, I may be right there with him. Whale hunting gets in your blood, I tell you, especially when you don't get any." Newman and Scott both mused that perhaps these whales had a sixth sense that alerted them to danger.

Only one whale ventured so close to the harpoon gun that it would have been almost impossible to miss—a jet-black minke who seemed fascinated by the hunting party. But minkes weren't killer whales—nor were they known as killers. They were, however, killer whale food. "We call her 'Minnie,'" wrote Scott. "It's a safe bet that no one has ever been this affectionate toward *Orcinus orca*." The whalers had a pet whale.

A few days after Scott's column was published, Sparrow had smaller fish to fry. He couldn't afford to miss halibut season and left the Gulf Islands to head out for the Bering Sea. Burich would now be the executioner. Newman and Penfold left too, along with the rest of the aquarium staff and the media. Newman recruited one of the aquarium's original volunteers, Joe Bauer, to work with Burich.

Bauer had been fishing since his childhood—first in Germany, which his family had made the mistake of visiting just as World War II broke out, leading to his father's internment at Dachau because of his anti-Nazi sentiments; then at a refugee camp in Scotland, where an old Gaelic fisherman taught him how to fish for herring; and later in Canada, where he studied fishing and net-making with First Nations fishermen. "I used to fish oolichans [candlefish] and was mentored by the Musqueam, the Stó:lō, and Tsawwassen bands," says Bauer. "They taught me a lot about respecting nature and working with nature rather than trying to dictate and control it." He was also taught to honor elders, offering them the pick of every catch. As a result of his respect for these traditions, as an adult Bauer was formally adopted by a Nisga'a family and received full First Nations status—including fishing rights—which he never used.

As a high school student in Steveston, a fishing and canning town just outside of Vancouver, Bauer collected exotic local fish for himself, then for the small aquarium run by UBC. His personal collection was almost as impressive as the university's; he had thirty tanks at home. "I had species UBC didn't even know existed," he says. UBC professor Dr. Wilbert Clemens was so impressed by the self-taught prodigy that Bauer became an aquarium fixture before there was an aquarium and was declared a lifetime member in 1956, while he was still in high school. Unable to afford university, Bauer worked as a fisherman but spent his spare time volunteering for Clemens and, later, Newman.

When the whaling expedition launched, the twenty-five-year-old Bauer was a diver and diving instructor (students included future Canadian environmental icon David Suzuki) and regularly helped the Canadian coast guard on rescue missions.

Bauer arrived on Saturna to search for other species for the aquarium and assist with the expedition, if necessary. He also brought a camera to chronicle the adventures. He knew Sparrow and Burich because they'd crossed paths as fishermen. It might be a big ocean, but it was a small community.

AFTER TEN DAYS, the coast guard crew left in response to reports of Russian whalers near the Queen Charlotte Islands (now known as Haida Gwaii), where they were believed to be venturing inside the three-mile fishing limit in their quest for whales much more valuable than killers.

Suddenly, Canada's biggest whale news was that Russians might harpoon the B.C. economy. Lorne Hume, general manager of Western Canadian Whaling, warned that local whalers could lose up to $2 million if the Soviets weren't stopped. They had four or five times as many boats as Hume had, as well as floating factory ships that allowed them to render whales on the water. According to Hume, "this could lead to a situation similar to that existing in Antarctica which has been so overhunted that whale biologists believe it will take 50 years for whales in that area to return to the number they were at before the Second World War." The Department of Fisheries sent a boat to photograph the Soviets to make sure they weren't violating international borders by killing whales that only Canadians were supposed to kill.

The circus had left Saturna. Only Burich and Bauer remained— and there were no killer whales in sight. It was as if the whales had read Scott's stories and decided to remove Saturna from their feeding route. Killer whales were spotted on May 22, 24, 26, and 28, but no new whales came close enough to shore to shoot. For almost an entire month—between May 28 and June 25—there were no sightings at all.

To fill the time, Burich taught Bauer how to use the harpoon and how to carve. The two amused themselves by etching their own twentieth-century petroglyphs of whales and whalers into the flat stones near their camp. They also made a flag displaying a killer whale and flew it over their tent. And they built a pen in a nearby bay where they could study the body of their whale after they caught and killed it, so that Bauer could take the photos and measurements.

For weeks, Burich played his harmonica, sculpted, and scraped images into the sandstone, while Bauer watched the water for whales and other species and collected a few exotic specimens for the aquarium's displays. They were both fishermen, so they knew how to wait or, to use the term preferred by fishermen, fish. Burich and Bauer would occasionally visit the Fletchers for company and the use of their shower.

ON JULY 15, after almost two months of waiting, Newman contacted Burich via ship-to-shore radio to call it a day. His whale hunt had become a snipe hunt. Instead of the pods of fifty-plus killers that had been recorded over the previous four years, only eight pods—a mere sixty whales—had been seen during Burich's fifty-seven days on the island. And whale season was winding down.

Burich still wanted his whale. His sculpture would be a tourist attraction that everyone in Vancouver and visitors from around the world would see. And, perhaps more importantly, he didn't want to let Newman down. But maybe Newman was right and the creatures could sense danger. After eight weeks, Burich agreed that it was time to abandon the quest.

That night, the Fletchers invited Burich and Bauer for a farewell dinner, and Pete broke out the homemade sake he'd been brewing. After a long night of swapping stories and sampling the potent rice wine, Burich and Bauer returned to their tent.

When they woke the morning of July 16, not only were both men hungover, they were cold. The hot summer weather had been replaced with an unseasonal chill, and the waves were choppy. For the first time since arriving, Burich and Bauer put on their coats as they prepared for their last breakfast on Saturna. It was a good time to be going.

Bauer had stopped shaving while he was on the island—he'd mentioned that he was a fan of Burich's fisherman's beard—but he wanted to clean up before returning home to his girlfriend. Burich, who looked like Ernest Hemingway in his bullfighting prime, decided his friend should keep the beard, grabbed Bauer's shaving gear, and hurled it off the cliff. "You want a shave," laughed Burich. "Go dive for it."

As Burich returned to their tent to finish packing and take down their flag, Bauer walked to the edge of the cliff to see where his shaving gear landed. It was sinking into the water—thirty-seven fathoms deep.

It was a good thing his girlfriend wasn't a fan of beards. "As I was standing there I see a group of whales coming right to where our harpoon gun was and I said, 'Sam, I think we've got a chance to get a whale.'"

Burich didn't even look outside the tent as he replied, "Bullshit."

There was no time to argue.

Bauer ran to the harpoon gun, filled it with gunpowder, stuffed in the capping, loaded the harpoon, and took aim. That's when Burich raced down the hill with Bauer's gear. "He's got my camera," says Bauer, "and he says 'I can't use this shit.'" Bauer, who was equally reluctant to use the harpoon, took his camera and scrambled for the perfect spot to shoot the scene. Burich scrambled for a spot to shoot the whale.

After weeks of practice, this was only Burich's second encounter with a live target—but that was one more shot than Bauer had taken.

The bigger whales seemed to sense trouble and swam just beyond the range of the harpoon. But one of the smaller ones stayed closer to shore and seemed to meet Burich's gaze.

Burich knew he could hit this beast. He had no choice. He braced for the recoil from the 1.5-ounce gunpowder charge, aimed at the waterline slightly ahead of the small whale, and pulled the trigger. Then the whale disappeared into the water. Burich was devastated. He reached for the line and started to haul it back in.

Bauer, who was perched on the bluff below, had a better view. Burich had hooked a whale.

Burich was sure Bauer was wrong, but Bauer was certain he'd seen the harpoon hit the killer. No matter what Bauer said, Burich wasn't convinced. He knew he'd missed.

When they pulled at the line, it seemed heavier than usual, almost taut. The debate was settled when the orange floats attached to it began flying toward the ocean. As the Scotchmen hit the water, there was no doubt—they had a whale on the hook. Burich shouted in triumph, "Oh my God, you're right." Their ears still ringing from the blast, the whalers sprinted to their boat, the *Corsair 2*.

Meanwhile, the lighthouse keepers shared the news with their fellow islanders. Everyone had been waiting for this moment—they all wanted to see the aquarium catch the creature. Roughly two dozen men, women, and children raced to East Point to see the dead whale. Some gathered on the beach, some arrived in small boats, and it seemed that all the men had rifles. "I never realized there were so many .303s on Saturna Island," says Bauer. "All of the sudden, the beach was full with all these people with all these guns."

Plan A was to kill the whale with a single shot from the harpoon, then drag the carcass to the pen.

It was time for Plan B—for Burich to shoot the orca with his rifle. If the harpoon hadn't killed it, his bullets would. The men watched in astonishment as the whale appeared. It wasn't moving—but two larger whales were holding it gingerly, keeping it afloat.

Burich and Bauer couldn't believe what they were seeing. When the American soldiers slaughtered whales in Iceland, they saw healthy whales approaching bloody ones and assumed they were arriving to tear their family members to shreds and feast on their remains. But instead of surfacing with strips of flesh in their mouths, these killers were supporting the injured whale. Instead of savagery, Burich and Bauer were witnessing compassion, empathy. Suddenly, the definitive killer whale textbooks had all the scientific value of *King Kong*.

The idea that killer whales might rescue each other was unimaginable. Yes, some people—including Burich and Bauer—knew these whales were related to dolphins. And they knew dolphins sometimes rescued each other and were even known to rescue humans. But these supersized dolphins were notorious for their brutality.

Although Burich and Bauer knew that these killer whales were capable of destroying anything in the water—especially their sixty-foot fishing boat—Bauer was convinced the whales were more interested in rescuing their wounded mate than attacking. Burich wasn't taking any chances, however, and as their boat approached the three whales, he locked, loaded, and leveled his rifle.

Were these whales protecting their companion from the men or from drowning? It didn't matter to Burich. He had a job to do. As soon as he was able to maneuver the boat close enough to his catch, he fired three shots. He was certain that at least two of his heavy-caliber bullets had hit their mark—but the whale didn't die. More surprisingly, it didn't attack. Neither did the larger whales.

That was when Bauer came up with Plan C.

"I told Sam, 'We've got to do something because there's something unusual happening here. If those two whales are helping, the animal's not in danger of dying, because otherwise they wouldn't be bothering with it.'"

Bauer untied the tiny lifeboat from the side of the *Corsair*, hopped in, and rowed toward the wounded whale. "Sam was petrified," says Bauer. "He thought that the whale was going to come to and the two that were helping were going to go after me. But all the years I fished out there with a skiff I'd had whales come up eyeball to eyeball to me and I never had any fear of them, eh? So I got a little close and Sam was just hollering, 'They're going to attack you! They're going to attack you!' Maybe I was too young or something, but I didn't fear the animal."

The islanders did. "They got furious and kept on yelling, 'They're gonna kill you, you'll get yourself killed,' because they figured that the whales were going to attack. But I had an altogether different feeling about it. When I saw the two other whales helping it, I couldn't understand why they would be considered killers," says Bauer. "They're busy helping their friend the same way that I am when I'm out at sea and helping somebody who needs it. So Sam stopped shooting."

Burich put down his gun, but the islanders kept firing.

Bauer was determined to save the whale. "I took the little plastic rowboat and got out between the whale and the guys onshore with the guns."

THE FIRST TIME Bauer saw a killer whale, he was only seven. The boat he was working on was chasing herring, and the whales were chasing the salmon following the herring. The captain told young Josef that killer whales were dangerous and that he had to be careful around them. But when one of the smallest members of the pod approached to have a look at the fishing boat, Bauer watched the whale instead of running from it. "I wasn't scared; I was fascinated."

As a diver who loved to take underwater photos, he'd encountered several killer whales over the years. Whenever they approached, Bauer's diving partners would race back to the boat, but Bauer kept snapping pictures. "I figure they can identify the difference between a human and a seal." A few close encounters on his seventeen-foot skiff convinced him the creatures might be curious about humans but not as a potential meal.

As Bauer approached their captive for a closer look, the two larger whales stayed with their injured mate. "I said, 'They're not going to attack me. They're not going to let that other whale drown.' So I got really quite close, because I wanted to see where the harpoon went." Bauer says it was a long time before he saw a puff pass through the harpooned whale's blowhole. It was alive. The larger whales moved away to allow it to swim, but they didn't move far.

The harpoon had gone through the whale's skin, just below the base of the skull, and it appeared to have struck blubber, not brains. In scientific terms, "The harpoon entered the left side of the body, just posterior to the calvarium and dorsal to the vertebral column, and passed completely through."

Bauer couldn't believe what he was seeing. "I hollered back at Sam, 'Phone Dr. Newman, I think we can have a live whale!'" But Bauer was just the assistant; Burich was the gunner, and he'd steered the *Corsair* toward his prey. He was close enough to finish the job. The small whale was breathing again, swimming on its own, and the two whales supporting it were fleeing the hunter and his boat. The wounded creature off East Point had to be eyeing the men as a potential meal. The idea that killer whales weren't lethal was illogical. Even if Bauer believed these creatures could tell the difference between humans and harbor seals, killers ate seals, sea lions, birds, horses, moose, and other whales—why wouldn't humans be on the menu? And why wouldn't the whales attack these men who had just attacked them? A wounded bear would attack, a wounded lion would attack—surely this wounded whale would be ferocious. Why wasn't it trying to topple Bauer's tiny boat?

Burich didn't have an answer, but now that he was so close that it would be impossible to miss his target, he didn't shoot. This time when the small killer whale looked him in the eye, he no longer saw a creature challenging him; he saw a confused, wounded animal wondering why someone had hurt him. Instead of delivering the coup de grace, Burich set down his rifle. This whale wasn't fatally injured and it wasn't attacking. And he'd just witnessed two other whales risk their lives to rescue it. Perhaps this whale needed to die—either for the aquarium's exhibit or to put it out of its misery—but not yet. "I just couldn't do it," he told reporters the next day. "It would have been an execution."

Burich hadn't killed a whale. He'd accidentally caught one.

Back onshore, the islanders lowered their guns and waited for the inevitable. When the wounded killer attacked the suicidal city slickers, they'd be there to save them. If it wasn't too late.

Instead of ramming the men and their small boat, however, the captive whale jumped, dove, rolled, and twisted—it was trying to shake loose the harpoon, not eat the harpoonist. As the whale tried to free itself, Burich called Newman from the ship-to-shore phone and explained that things hadn't gone quite according to plan.

Newman couldn't believe what he was hearing. A live killer whale? It wasn't possible. But if it was true, if this whale was stuck on the line, his aquarium and his career would never be the same.

For the next three hours, the whale kept diving, twisting, turning, and leaping in an attempt to shake the harpoon loose—but it never threatened its awestruck captors.

Burich and Bauer steered away from East Point toward Fiddler's Cove, where they'd set up their pen. When the whale swam into a bed of kelp near some of the islanders in their boats, it let loose a series of shrill whistles. It seemed upset. Burich and Bauer navigated back toward the ocean, settling about three hundred feet offshore—away from the islanders and their rifles. As their captive calmed down and stopped howling, the two men and their whale waited for Ahab.

CHAPTER FIVE

THE TERRIBLE STRUGGLE

"So little was known about Orcinus Orca. Its mouthful of imposing teeth and ability to hunt intelligently in packs, caused most people to speak in awe of the mammal. A cross-section picture of a Great White Shark and a mad ship-ramming Sperm Whale usually emerged in the telling of stories. Tales of Arctic explorers on ice packs being attacked by frenzied killer whales and small boats being capsized were commonplace. Scuba divers feared them, and would leave the water when a whale was sighted."

PETE FLETCHER, *TIMES COLONIST*, MARCH 8, 1992

PETE FLETCHER KNEW that Burich and Bauer were doomed. When Pat McGeer's floatplane arrived from Vancouver, Fletcher warned him of "a terrible struggle." Like everyone else, Fletcher knew what these killer whales were capable of: he'd seen them swallow seals and sea lions. It was only a matter of time before the monster on the end of the harpoon line regained its senses and temper, smashed the tiny fishing boat, and tore Burich and Bauer to shreds. This was a killer whale, after all.

McGeer, the only member of the hunting party who knew nothing about whales beyond the apparent weight of their gray matter, took in the scene with a cold, scientific eye. He considered the size of the creature on the end of the line and the size of the *Corsair* and concluded that yes, this whale could absolutely destroy the boat— and that meant one thing. If the whale wanted to kill the men, they'd already be dead. "It was swimming behind the boat," says McGeer. "You only had to look and not have your mind contaminated by previous nonsense."

McGeer convinced Fletcher to ferry him out to the *Corsair*.

Burich and Bauer didn't want to kill their captive. Now that they'd both been close enough to determine that the whale's wounds were superficial, they weren't sure whether to cut it loose or find a way to lead it back to the big city. But neither one wanted to shoot it again. After trying, and failing, to shake loose the harpoon, the most feared creature on the planet was swimming a few feet from their boat and looking—kind of cute.

But McGeer was the boss. If the aquarium's lead scientist wanted Burich to pump a few more bullets into their captive, it was his call. That was the job they'd signed on for.

McGeer had never seen a killer whale before and, as he examined the creature in the water, didn't see a killer whale in front of him now. He saw a golden opportunity. If a dead whale was worth dissecting, a live whale could be invaluable. "There was this whale just swimming docilely behind the boat, so I said, 'Don't shoot it, for heaven's sake, we'll just wait and decide what to do.'"

As the three men waited, McGeer started to imagine the tests he could run, the tests everyone could run. No one had seen one of these animals up close before. They could use electrocardiograms to listen to the heart, electroencephalographs to study the internal organs, hydrophones to record the squeaks and squeals...

McGeer had only joined the expedition for one reason—the chance to examine one of the world's biggest and most complicated brains. But he could wait to slice into the huge skull. Instead of studying the whale's brain, he could keep the killer alive and study its intelligence. He looked at the whale on the end of the six-hundred-foot nylon tether and mused aloud, "I wonder what that thing is thinking with *my* brain." Bauer still suspected McGeer wanted the dead brain more than he wanted the live whale.

It was all up to Newman.

Soon they heard the buzz of another floatplane. The whale must have heard it too. As the men looked up at the sky, the whale slid underwater, presumably to escape the sound. As Newman arrived to meet his crew, all he saw was the boat. Then the monster surfaced.

Newman had never seen a killer up close, but he'd read all the literature and he'd been warned by the experts—he knew how risky this enterprise was.

Haunted by visions of the ill-fated Marineland expedition, Newman worried that his men were risking their lives, that he was risking their lives. His hunters weren't as well-armed as Marineland's, who needed ten bullets from a .357 Magnum to stop a killer. The whale expert at the British Natural History Museum had also regaled Newman with horror stories about these vicious predators. What if this wounded beast toppled the boat or an angry mate rammed it? A live whale would be a coup for his aquarium, but a dead crew...

Newman was the captain. If his ship was going down, he'd go down with it. He asked the pilot to land beside his boat. The pilot was probably as enthusiastic about delivering his passengers to the boat as Fletcher had been. What if this monster charged the floatplane? But this was a Department of Fisheries flight and Newman wasn't the only person on board. Bob McLaren—one of the department bosses—was in the other seat, and he wanted to see a whale.

The moment Newman received Burich's call, he started weighing his options. Before boarding the floatplane, Newman asked Kathy for advice. "You have to kill it," she told him. She worried that if her husband brought a wounded creature back to the big city and it died in front of the media, the bad publicity could sink the aquarium.

Should he follow Kathy's advice—which he usually did—stick to the plan, and put the whale out of its misery? With a few well-placed bullets, Newman could declare his expedition a smashing success.

They could kill the whale and drag the corpse to the harbor, Bauer could take photos and measurements and deliver the body to the scientists waiting to dissect it, and Burich could start sculpting. That was what his board, the media, and the people of the province were expecting. But when Newman saw the creature up close, he wondered whether he could really order Burich to kill it.

The whale wasn't attacking and didn't appear to have much interest in Newman or his men. It was swimming slowly beside the boat—probably exhausted—making the occasional dip and dive as it tried to dislodge the metal prong. As soon as Newman boarded the Corsair, he saw why Burich and Bauer wanted to save this whale. "There was this beautiful black and white animal, which was assumed to be very dangerous and now was clearly an animal that needed help and no longer seemed terribly dangerous." The boy who had been fascinated by trout was now the man looking at the most majestic creature in the oceans.

When the whale swam closer, it was as clear to Newman as it had been to Bauer that the injury was almost impossibly minor—the harpoon had gone straight through the blubber, and a single good slice would sever the line. This whale's family had survived worse. Almost a quarter of the whales in the Salish Sea were scarred by gunshots from fishermen or the military; some had bullets lodged in their blubber. Larger whales swam the open sea with their bodies still holding the remnants of ancient harpoons. Should Newman's crew cut the nylon line and let their captive loose?

How would he explain that to anyone other than the men on the Corsair? And how would he live with himself if he had the greatest marine exhibit of all time on the line and let it go? Should his crew attempt to take their captive back to the city, do what Marineland couldn't—and what no one else could imagine daring—and become the envy of every other aquarium on the planet?

McGeer knew what he wanted and made the case. This miracle whale was a scientific gold mine. "Murray and I are not brave," says McGeer. "So we were appropriately cautious, but there were events unfolding right in front of us, so you act on those."

Newman stared at the whale, waiting for a sign of the vicious behavior that would make his decision easy. "You can imagine that if this had been a lion or a tiger or something on the end of a rope it would be a furious, savage contest, the animal will be right at you," said Newman. "We thought it would turn and attack us like a wounded bear."

Like the men on the boat, the whale waited for Newman to make a decision.

Newman always publicly and privately credited McGeer's passion with convincing him to save the whale. But from the moment Burich called to relay the message that he and Bauer had hooked a live, healthy killer and it just might be possible to take it home, it's hard to imagine that a man who was fascinated by every living creature he'd ever seen—from herring to hawks—could make any other decision. His whalers had accidentally captured Moby Dick. How could he resist bringing it home? As Newman and his crew discussed their next move, the mini-Moby swam at the end of the line—never pulling it taut—as it called out to its family, either asking for help or warning them that here be dragons.

IF NEWMAN WAS going to keep this creature, he had to find somewhere to put it. He knew exactly where a killer whale was supposed to fit in his aquarium—hanging from the rafters and dangling above the awestruck visitors. There would be plenty of room on his ceiling, but he certainly didn't have a tank big enough to display a whale.

The most obvious choice was Lost Lagoon—a forty-one-acre artificial lake in the same park as the aquarium. There was plenty of space for a whale to swim, much more space than Marineland had for its pilot whales—but the water was shallow and brackish and the lagoon was extremely public, located right next to a highway in downtown Vancouver.

Vancouver's Jericho Beach might work. It was on the ocean, and there was an old military base there—but no natural pool. It would take weeks, maybe months, to build a pen that could corral the creature.

McGeer suggested a naval dry dock on nearby Vancouver Island. It was about the same distance from Saturna as Vancouver, and as a politician, he could pull the required strings to get the navy to open its gates. The only problem—the Vancouver Aquarium wasn't on Vancouver Island, and if Newman was going to save this whale, he was taking it home. The idea of a dry dock—a facility designed to store and repair ships—was perfect. But what about a dry dock near Vancouver?

Thanks to his adventures with H.R. MacMillan, Newman knew the general manager of Burrard Yarrows Dry Dock, David Wallace— not well, but well enough to make a call. Newman reached Wallace, who was at a cocktail party, from the *Corsair's* radio. "We've just captured this killer whale, and I was wondering if we could keep it at your dry dock for a few days." Newman also reminded Wallace that they'd been introduced by their mutual friend "H.R."—dropping the heaviest name in western Canada. Wallace couldn't quite believe what he was hearing. He knew about the crazy quest to kill a whale— it was front-page news—but this request was so off the wall that he thought Newman had to be kidding. But Newman made it clear that this was serious and only Wallace could save the day.

Wallace offered to lend Newman a berth. Then Newman mentioned that the aquarium had no money to pay for the whale's lodgings, and Wallace was suddenly all business. The whale could stay—but only until Monday. It was Thursday night. Wallace was happy to help, but he was not interested in turning away paying customers. As dusk fell, Newman, McGeer, and McLaren left to prepare a whale pen and alert the world that the Vancouver Aquarium had made history.

BURICH AND BAUER had to figure out how to get their captive to come with them without injuring it any further, and the dry dock was more than thirty miles away. Under normal circumstances, in decent weather, the boat would be able to make it to Vancouver in about two hours. They could be at the dry dock in less than three.

But there was nothing normal about this trip. They didn't want to risk doing any more damage to the whale, and they couldn't put any strain on the line without ripping it out of the orca's flesh and losing, harming, or perhaps even killing their captive.

Burich and Bauer stared at the listless creature swimming by their side and tried to figure out how to make the move as painless as possible. There had to be a way to cushion their catch from the inevitable bumps as they traveled through the waves. As fishermen, Burich and Bauer were used to solving problems at sea. Bauer borrowed an old car tire, and they tied it to their line to create a shock absorber to minimize any pain for the whale and avoid aggravating the injury.

After determining the speed at which the whale seemed comfortable swimming—roughly two knots (a little over two miles per hour)—the trio started toward Vancouver. The whale soon settled on its preferred spot for the trip—three hundred feet astern and slightly to starboard. Burich and Bauer believed the whale chose this position as the best way to avoid irritating the wound. As daylight faded—along with the shock of what they'd done—they felt it was less like having a killer on the end of the line than a dog on a leash. And now that their captive had become their companion, it needed a name. Although the Beatles were taking over the teenaged world, for adults this was still the age of Elvis. Burich dubbed the killer Hound Dog.

The pair kept a close eye on Hound Dog to make sure it was doing okay. They took turns steering, and roughly every four minutes, when Hound Dog would surface, one of them would time the breathing. They monitored the rhythms to make sure their whale was as comfortable as possible.

"The whale was not towed," says Bauer, who cringed when he read news reports the next day that referred to "towing" the whale. "It was led. That's why it took us so long to get across, because we went the speed the whale was able to travel at. We were watching the whale all the time and we never once tightened the line. You're not going to keep an animal alive and tow it. It's an air-breathing animal like we are."

Burich also balked at reports that they had towed the whale and told CBC TV, "We didn't actually tow her; we more or less led her—like a puppy dog on a leash."

They weren't the only ones watching out for Hound Dog's well-being. Another whale, probably one of the two that had saved it from drowning, followed at a safe distance. The humans watching the whale speculated that it was their captive's mate. Some First Nations believed killer whales mate for life—likely based on the fact that the family units are virtually inseparable. But orcas aren't grand romantics. Orcas mate when they intermingle with other pods. The strongest bond for an orca isn't with its mate but with its mom. The whale following Hound Dog was most likely to be its mother, or possibly one of the older females charged with babysitting.

As the group traveled across the Strait of Georgia, news spread across Canada as quickly as it had across Saturna. CBC TV reported that "a five-ton killer whale had the tables turned tonight, after a long, dangerous battle with a team from the Vancouver Aquarium. The giant whale was harpooned this afternoon near Saturna Island... The men had to pump three bullets from a hunting rifle into the huge, gray shape before the whale showed signs of tiring. The aquarium director, Murray Newman, flew to the scene later to assist in towing the pugnacious, dangerous monster to shore... It was photographed and will be dissected by marine scientists."

The news that the aquarium had a whale was out. But initial media reports indicated that the original plan was unchanged and that the hunters were only taking their catch to Vancouver to dissect it. One reporter with the scoop on the new mission to save the whale was the *Vancouver Sun*'s Terry Hammond, who wrote that "ironically, the two men who braved the elements for 10 weeks trying to kill a killer spent Thursday night battling choppy seas, blinding squalls and darkness to save their victim's life."

Bauer says the weather wasn't that bad, but he had spent his life on the water—and wasn't trying to sell newspapers. As the hunters and their catch approached the city, the coast guard joined them for the last part of the journey. "The *Chilco Post* acted as an escort as we got close to Vancouver—mainly to ensure that other craft didn't get in the way or become entangled in the line," says Bauer. "There were a lot of curious people wanting to see the captive." The coast guard crew that was originally supposed to finish off the killer was serving as the whale's security detail.

After eighteen hours of nonstop travel, Burich, Bauer, and the "pugnacious, dangerous monster," finally reached Vancouver harbor. The men were exhausted, but Hound Dog appeared to be fine—or as fine as an orca could be after being pierced by a harpoon, repeatedly shot, and forced to take an eighteen-hour trip across the ocean.

The whale following the boat took one last look at the orca who was probably her child and swam away from the crowd that was waiting for them. Minutes later, Burich, Bauer, and Hound Dog were greeted by a flotilla of Sunday sailors hoping for a glimpse of the impossible—a captive killer whale.

Despite the care taken in transporting the whale, it still had a sharp metal spike lodged underneath its skin, salt water was washing an open wound, and the creature had lost its family, its home, its world. The young orca, who had spent its entire life within a few feet of its mother, was suddenly, for the first time, completely alone.

CHAPTER SIX

THE PUGNACIOUS, DANGEROUS MONSTER

"And now, ladies and gentlemen, before I tell you any more, I'm going to show you the greatest thing your eyes have ever beheld. He was a king and a god in the world he knew, but now he comes to civilization merely a captive—a show to gratify your curiosity. Ladies and gentlemen, look at Kong, the Eighth Wonder of the World."

KING KONG, 1933

I T TRULY WAS as if Burich had harpooned King Kong, the Sasquatch, or an extraterrestrial. This was what UFO researchers would have dubbed a "close encounter of the third kind"—first contact with an alien species. At 11:30 AM on Friday, July 17, 1964—just over twenty-four hours after Burich landed his whale—the *Corsair* and the killer passed under Vancouver's iconic Lions Gate Bridge, and the world met the pugnacious, dangerous monster.

The front-page banner headline of the morning edition of the *Vancouver Sun* exclaimed: "Wounded Whale Swims in on Leash." The story began: "A harpooned, bullet-wounded killer whale was led into Vancouver harbor on a leash today, all in the interests of science. Vancouver Aquarium Society officials decided to bring it here after amateur hunters failed to kill it following the five-ton

55

mammal's capture Thursday morning." The *Sun* reported that the whale was fifteen feet long. The front page of its rival daily, the *Province*, announced that the "voracious prowler of the north Pacific" was twenty feet long. Like all the best fish stories, the size shifted based on who was doing the telling. So did almost all the other details. The *Province* also told readers the whale had been brought to Vancouver to be slaughtered—news that did not sit well with officials at the SPCA.

By the time Burich and Bauer navigated to the dry dock, thousands of people had crowded the shoreline to witness history. Wallace assigned nine workers to help Burich, Bauer, and other aquarium volunteers transfer the whale into its new home. Dozens of other dockworkers watched as two men in a box dangling from a crane maneuvered the whale into the dry dock. The men had moved exotic cargo before, but this was their first live passenger, and it wasn't cooperating. After the whale was herded into the dry dock, the crane operators steered it into a holding pen, then raised the water level to make their captive more comfortable. The killer initially responded to its new surroundings with a slap of the tail- and observers assumed it was scared—but after the aquarium's assistant curator, Vince Penfold, dislodged the harpoon from the whale's back, it stopped struggling.

Says McGeer: "Once it was in the dry dock, it was not a job at all to remove the harpoon that was holding the animal, so it was turned into a domestic creature in a matter of hours." Although the harpoon was gone, the looped nylon rope that had passed through the whale's flesh was left intact. The plan was to use it as a leash to lead the whale to its next home. Almost as soon as the harpoon was gone, the whale started swimming counterclockwise in its new home, which ranged from seven to thirteen feet deep.

A CBC radio reporter brought recording equipment, dropped it underwater, and made broadcast history when the station shared the creature's strange sounds with networks around the world. It was the first time most people on the planet had heard the calls of a killer whale—or any whale. The National Film Board cameraman Jack Long, who'd shot the start of the expedition on Saturna, arrived to finish his newsreel.

When the media finally interviewed Burich about the shot that had hooked Hound Dog, Burich replied like a seasoned whaler: "I just let her have it." He also quipped, "Now can I have a free pass to the aquarium?" Newman responded by offering him a new job instead—as the whale's caretaker. Burich would receive $300 a month—the same salary he'd been promised for sculpting the whale—to spend eight hours a day watching it. His job was to keep the killer company, earn its trust, and, most importantly, find a way to feed it.

Now that the specimen was in its goldfish bowl, Newman wanted it left alone to recover. He knew the only other killer in captivity had survived less than forty-eight hours, and he didn't want to risk losing his prize—especially in front of the public. Newman knew his wife was right—this dream could easily turn into a disaster. "It was front-page news," said Newman. "It was in all the media all over the world. Everybody wanted to know about it."

Newman believed that if his whale survived the first seventy-two hours in the dry dock, it would live another decade or more. Although no one had a clue how long a killer whale lived, they figured it must be at least a dozen years, maybe twenty, and Hound Dog appeared to be young. So the first order of business was to figure out how to keep a whale alive.

Wallace didn't care that the world was watching. He quickly saw that there was no way he could host the world's biggest celebrity and run his business. From the moment Hound Dog swam into the harbor, Wallace's men had stopped working and started gawking.

Everyone else wanted to see the whale too. After some people were caught climbing the fence to catch a glimpse of the monster, Wallace hired full-time security guards from Pinkerton's to keep intruders out of his shipyard.

The day the whale arrived, the *Nanaimo Daily Free Press* ran an unrelated story quoting local scientist Gordon Pike, sharing his frustration at the failure of a global whale conservation accord. Pike (who had dibs on dissecting Hound Dog's organs) warned that without an agreement to limit the number of whales that could be harvested, B.C.'s rendering plant at Coal Harbour couldn't survive for long, and at the rate Japanese, Norwegian, and Russian factory ships were slaughtering the species, neither could whales.

NEWMAN AND MCGEER contacted everyone they could think of who might be able to help with the care and feeding of a killer whale, including UBC's dean of medicine. The whale's initial medical staff included a heart specialist, a bacteriologist, a mammalogist, a dermatologist, and a vet. "We called in everybody but a psychiatrist," jokes McGeer, "and nobody was too busy to help."

The prey became the patient. But even though the whale just kept swimming in slow circles, the scientists were still concerned it might try to kill them as soon as it regained its senses. "We really didn't know what the whale was going to do," said Newman. "We thought that maybe the animal was just stunned."

Since the whale had been hit by a harpoon—and shot several times—there was a decent chance of an infection, and McGeer wanted to treat the whale with antibiotics. He attempted to feed Hound Dog a dead salmon by lowering it into the dock on a long fishing line, and he used the classic veterinarian's trick of stuffing the food with medicine. Just like any other hound, the whale sniffed at the supplement-laced salmon and swam away. McGeer would have to devise another way to protect his patient from potential infection.

Although Bauer was certain Hound Dog was male—he was convinced he had seen a penis when he rowed the lifeboat out to meet the whale—the senior scientists disagreed. Based on the size of the whale, the shape of its dorsal fin, and the mammary glands, the scientists and whale experts believed not only that Hound Dog was female, but also, since this was breeding season, that there was a 30 percent chance she was pregnant. McGeer relayed this information to the media, and although there was still some doubt about the whale's gender, reporters latched onto the idea that the whale was "a lady." Over the next few days, aquarium staff upped the odds of pregnancy to fifty-fifty.

McGeer decided to hold off on his tests until Hound Dog had time to adjust to her new surroundings. For the sake of science, McGeer wanted a resting heartbeat—and he didn't want to disturb his patient any more than was necessary. Both McGeer and Newman knew that the whale needed rest to recover, but it also needed a home for longer than Wallace was prepared to keep it. McGeer says Newman convinced Wallace to hold a one-day open house so that the world could meet the whale.

On Saturday, July 18—the day after the whale arrived in Vancouver—huge crowds braved the rain to line up to see the world's most exotic exhibit.

NINE-YEAR-OLD JOHN FORD was delighted when his dad announced they were going to the dry dock. A killer whale—this would be worth standing in line with a bunch of grown-ups and getting drenched by the rain. Ford vividly remembered a trip on the family speed boat a few years earlier when he and his parents barely survived a close call with these beasts. A pod of killer whales stalked them, swimming toward their fifteen-foot boat and then right underneath it.

"We were all terrified," Ford says, "including my father. These were wolves of the sea; they would eat anything, including people, without hesitation. If they bumped the boat, and we tipped over, we'd be consumed right away. So we were all gripping the gunnels of the boat." The Ford family braced for the worst. "The whales, of course, passed, and that was that."

But this was different. Now the whale was in the boy's world, and his father was taking him to get a glimpse of the legendary creature. "I had my very first Brownie camera—a little box with a trigger. You look at the image in the viewfinder upside down and backwards." He caught a photo of a fin but not much more. "It was a peekaboo view," says Ford, who was surprised the monster didn't look more like a monster.

"It didn't seem so impressive because it was a big dry dock and a very small whale, sort of looking rather lonely in there. It certainly didn't seem to be very dangerous from my young boy's perspective. It was fascinating—but I don't think it really struck me as being an animal that was dangerous if you got close to it. And it didn't seem to be showing any behavior that would be dangerous to people who were standing around the edge of the enclosure."

This lack of aggressiveness was a huge relief for Newman, who knew the whale was capable of making a meal out of any tourist who got too close.

For a nine-year-old, the crowd was more overwhelming than the whale.

The dry dock staff allowed roughly five hundred people in at a time, and estimates of the total number of visitors ranged up to twenty thousand—almost the same number that would see the Beatles in Vancouver a few months later. "There was probably a little less screaming and fainting around the whale than there was around the Beatles," says Ford. "It wasn't quite Orcamania like it was Beatlemania."

Another visitor, Oliver Gates, told reporters: "I was very disappointed and so were other people I talked to there. It was much smaller than I expected and it wasn't very interesting to just stand there and watch it swim around."

The whole scene was like a classic movie about first contact with an alien or a monster. What happens when it arrives? Everyone panics, the villagers break out their guns and torches, and they either kill it or capture it and put the alien on display. Before he escaped and climbed the Empire State Building, King Kong was chained in a Broadway theater, surrounded by showgirls. Just as the captive Kong appeared harmless, once people saw a killer whale up close— trapped in our world—the ancient fear of the apex predator began to evaporate. The wolf of the sea had become the ocean's cuddly kitty. The grizzly was now a panda.

THE SPCA WAS outraged about the capture of the whale. Unless it wasn't. On the front page of the *Province* the day the whale arrived in the city, Vancouver SPCA president Dennis Price declared, "If this is what the aquarium is for, I don't think we need it."

Price told the newspaper he was appalled by what the aquarium was doing to the captive whale—or at least what he'd been told the aquarium was doing—dragging the harpooned captive to the city before putting it out of its misery. "It's nothing else but cruelty," said Price, who promised the SPCA would protest. "It's sadistic to let an animal suffer all that time. I'm sure there could have been a quicker way to at least render the whale senseless. If they must have a whale they should have used methods which would kill it instantly."

It's possible Price's outrage was prompted by a legitimate error on the reporter's part. It's also possible the *Province* was manufacturing outrage because, until this point, their rivals at the *Sun* had owned the whale story, courtesy of Jack Scott's visit to Saturna. Either way, the *Province* successfully launched a controversy about captivity that hasn't died down since 1964. The *Sun*, which reported that the whale was being brought to the city to be studied—not shot—also featured a quote from B.C. SPCA president David Beeching vowing to investigate whether the whale was suffering and declaring the capture "crazy." Kathy Newman was right when she warned that not everyone was going to be pleased that her husband had landed his great black-and-white whale.

There was no controversy when the aquarium had announced the hunt for the whale in May or when a machine gun was set up in B.C. waters to kill as many killer whales as possible. Complaints at Marineland were more likely to be about the cost of admission or snacks than the conditions of the whales. But the image of a harpooned whale being "towed" into the harbor to be slaughtered in a dry dock launched a new era in animal rights advocacy.

Canada's original anti-captivity activist—perhaps the world's—was Florence Barr. Well known to politicians and media, Barr was a former president of the Vancouver SPCA, and she started a petition to ask Canada's minister of fisheries, James Sinclair, to order the aquarium to free the whale. She fired her initial salvo at Sinclair in a terse telegram: "Strongly protest cruelty to whale by your department at Vancouver. Request termination of experiments. Petition follows." Her petition wasn't likely to find favor with Sinclair, who'd visited Saturna to watch the hunt.

Unlike other SPCA officials, Barr had not been inspired to act by misinformation. If the media had been looking for someone to oppose the initial hunt—nevermind the capture—she would certainly have obliged. Barr was especially upset about the idea of displaying the whale to the public like a sideshow exhibit. "It's just terrible the way they've treated this creature," she said. "Thousands of people gaping at it, a rope in its side—it's simply terrible." She told the Province: "Those scientists should be taken out and harpooned for what they are doing to the whale—I was horrified that all those people could go down and stare at the whale and not do anything to help it."

CBC TV described Barr as a fanatic—an accusation that predated her interest in whales. She and her husband, Captain James Barr, were veteran animal rights campaigners who'd arrived in Canada from Glasgow in 1924. James, who worked as an employment services officer, was a key player in introducing more humane procedures to Vancouver's slaughterhouses in the 1920s. In the 1930s, Florence fought to improve conditions at Vancouver's pig farms and spearheaded a law that made it illegal for dogs to travel on the running boards of cars. It should have been no surprise to anyone when she began lobbying to save the whale.

Barr told the Victoria Daily Times: "It's perfectly awful to keep that thing alive and have it suffer like that. It makes me shudder that no one is rising up to protest the treatment it has received... A whale is a very intelligent mammal—it suffers just like a human being. It's no different than keeping a man with a spear in his back in captivity."

Barr declared Vancouverites "a bunch of savages" for not fighting to free the whale. Judging by B.C.'s newspapers, there were others who thought Barr had a point. In a letter to the *Colonist*, Tom Taylor wrote that after the whale was studied, it should be set free and not "sold like a slave for ignorant adults like yours truly to gawk at. She is too valuable as a scientific treasure and will have her heart and brain read, presumably to see what makes her tick. But after that, after she has satisfied marine curiosity and titillated the Vancouver scene, deserves to be set free."

One *Sun* reader voiced his concerns about "what disgusting hokum goes on in the name of science." Another wrote to ask, "Is there no authority in this highly regimented world to prevent people from playing at useless research while inflicting untold tortures on a defenseless animal?"

WHILE MCGEER LED the team of volunteer scientists and veterinarians who were trying to examine the whale's behavior and tend to its wounds, Newman worked the phones trying to find a more permanent home for his prize catch. He didn't just want to save the whale; he was determined to keep it.

Newman joined the son-in-law of his benefactor H.R. to scout potential locations. In his autobiography, Newman wrote, "We drove around the North Shore looking for a place where we were going to develop a facility. We looked at the old cannery—that was a very good location—and we could've bought the whole thing for $250,000, which then seemed like a huge amount of money." Creating a new space for the whale was even more expensive. Newman told the media it would probably cost $500,000 to build a proper home for the whale—$200,000 more than it had cost to build the aquarium—and it was impossible to create a viable tank in a few days.

That's when Marineland's curator, David Brown, offered a solution. While other aquarists and researchers from around the world called and sent telegrams to congratulate Newman, Brown made an offer. He wanted to take the whale to Hollywood. After all, Marine-land already had pilot whales—it could handle a killer whale.

When Brown asked how much the aquarium wanted to part with its prize, Newman answered $20,000, a price he hoped would sound outrageously high. "I just pulled the number out of my head," said Newman. Brown called his bluff. If the whale was healthy, he'd write the check. Newman backpedaled and told Brown he wasn't interested.

Newman knew that if he didn't find a home for the whale soon, he'd have no choice but to sell it, so he called in the cavalry. Naturally, he knew some military leaders, courtesy of his friendship with H.R., and contacted his fishing buddy Stevie—Air Vice-Marshal Leigh Stevenson—to help approach the chief of staff at the military base across Vancouver harbor. Colonel William "Bull" Matthews agreed to transform the army's seaplane dock into a makeshift research center—a seventy-five-by-forty-foot armor-plated pen, with sides made from old fencing wire and a bottom built from the steel mesh used to construct emergency airfields. Since there was no budget, it would be built by volunteers from the aquarium, the dry dock, and the army. Eighty military men offered to help. They couldn't have the new space ready by Monday, as Wallace wanted, but they were certain it could be ready for the whale by Wednesday.

The proposed pen was front-page news. CBC TV reported that "a special pen will be built for the distinguished captive at Jericho Beach. The whale is now staying at Burrard Drydock in North Van-couver where the prize specimen went on private display for the first time." In less than forty-eight hours, the "pugnacious, dangerous monster" had become a "distinguished captive" and "prize specimen."

Meanwhile, the whale kept swimming in the same lazy circles, crying out for her family and refusing to eat.

CHAPTER SEVEN

SUPERPOD

"The whale made noises all night long and I listened. I wished I knew what he was trying to say. Did he try to tell me about his sorrow for his dead mate, about his loneliness, or were these just meaningless sounds? I had a strong feeling that this big whale was an intelligent being with a man-sized brain, who didn't speak man's language. He'd come up from the depth of the sea to confront man. The day may come when man will confront different looking creatures on other planets and it'll probably be the same. How are we going to tell if it's a beast or something like we are with passion and compassion? I wished I knew."

NAMU, THE KILLER WHALE

WHEN HOUND DOG'S family, now known as J pod, meets one or both of the other two pods identified as southern resident killer whales (SRKW), the orcas from each community line up side by side and face each other. It looks as if they're entering into a military formation, like ancient warriors or fighter jets preparing for a strafing run—and much like the scene Marineland's capture crew encountered that convinced them to free a baby whale rather than risk the wrath of the vengeful monsters.

Human groups who find themselves hunting in the same territory are almost expected to fight. For the most part, regardless of the
continent they're on or their culture, it's rare when they don't battle
over land or resources. But the orca culture is more ancient than ours
and, apparently, more civilized. Killer whales don't just share food;
they share the same sectors of the seas without challenging each
other to determine dominance. This is true for orca families found in
every ocean in the world. But in aquarium tanks, orcas from different
pods, and different parts of the planet, have sparred for supremacy
or space. In these cramped quarters, the whales will attack each
other—something they've almost never been seen doing in the wild
(though there is one known instance where it appeared residents
chased Bigg's whales away from a newborn). Orcas in the ocean
don't hurt each other, even though they're certainly capable of it.

Instead of attacking whales from other pods, when the southern
residents meet, the groups perform a ritual that may date back a million years. They approach, posture, pass each other, and then—for
lack of a better word—they dance. Certainly from a human's view-
point, the militaristic ritual appears to shift into a celebration. The
orcas party, they mate, and the older females who lead each of the
clans cluster and, despite the difference in their dialects, appear to
discuss... something.

Food? Families? Fertility? Orca politics?

When the orcas meet, the gatherings are called superpods.

Ken Balcomb is fascinated by the way the older females from
each pod gather when they cross paths. Balcomb finds it so clear that
the creatures are communicating that he imagines thought balloons
over their heads, like they're characters in a comic book. When he
watches superpods, Balcomb is reminded of the ancient potlatch cer-
emonies practiced by the Salish Sea's First Nations. He has no doubt
that what he's watching in the ocean is an ancient culture, honoring
ancient traditions.

Early orca researchers were surprised to discover that killer
whales mature at roughly the same rate as humans. Babies nurse

for a year, and the species doesn't become sexually active until their teens. But the real shock was the discovery that female orcas live beyond their reproductive age. There are only two species besides humans in which females are known to experience a significant postmenopausal life—short-finned pilot whales and orcas (the two largest delphinids). Even female elephants and great apes don't live long after they're no longer fertile, but female orcas live for decades, perhaps more than half a century, after menopause.

Not long after people began figuring out how to identify individual orcas, one of the whales in the Salish Sea made a serious impression on researchers because of her apparent age. Scientists believed the whale numbered J2, which Balcomb named Granny, was postmenopausal, or senescent, when she was first identified by humans after being captured, then released, in the late 1960s. Based on her relationship with J1—the senior male of her pod, who researchers surmised was either her son or her brother—the best guess was that Granny was born in 1911, the same year workers finished crafting the invulnerable hull of the *Titanic*, three years before the outbreak of World War I. In 1964, Granny was one of J pod's designated babysitters. In orca culture, the senior females not only lead the packs but also care for and educate the youngsters while their mother searches for fish that will be shared with their child and the elder. One of the senior female members of J pod would have had the best chance of rescuing the drowning juvenile harpooned off Saturna. If Granny was born in 1911, she would have been too old to be the mother but the right age to be the grandmother or caretaker. If Granny was born closer to 1936, as some scientists suspect, she may have been the captive whale's mother.

The evolutionary theory behind the survival of the orca matriarchs is known as "the grandmother hypothesis," which posits that serving as a wise and revered elder in this society is more valuable to the survival of the species than birthing more babies. Matriarchs survive to care for and protect young whales and to pass on wisdom—like the intricacies of the language, the boundaries of their traditional territories, where to find food in tough times, and how to avoid danger.

A killer whale's gestation period is fifteen to eighteen months, mothers can die in childbirth, only sixty percent of babies survive their first year, and oceans can only support so many apex predators, so families are small. If it takes a village to raise a child, it takes a pod—and a grandmother—to raise an orca. There's a language to learn, a huge hunting area to explore, secrets to share. Orcas will even act as midwives to usher in new members of the pod. There's evidence of orcas assisting in a breach birth by pulling the baby loose from the mother with their teeth—and gripping the newborn gently enough to avoid harming it.

Perhaps because grannies rule, orcas are famous for their empathy. They care for each other's offspring, they care for each other, and they don't just catch food together, they share their catch—even in bad times. Some researchers wonder whether this commitment to caring proves that empathy provides an evolutionary advantage. Orcas have been around a lot longer than we have. Killer whales appear to have been roaming and ruling our oceans for roughly 6 million years. Humans have only been around for 200,000. Of course, it's also possible that these creatures we once dismissed as monsters are just nicer than we are. Unlike many species noted for their intelligence, orca clans are tightly knit, with pods sharing the same dialects and the same hunting grounds. Families don't split up to start new pods, and males not only remain beside their mothers but rarely survive for more than a few years after their mother's death.

Older female orcas don't just lead their clans in their never-ending search for food; they serve as matchmakers. They also engage in foreplay with visiting males from other pods to get them in the mood for mating, before introducing them to the fertile females. They may even have fun with the visiting males themselves before they make the introductions—like other delphinids, orcas enjoy recreational sex.

Biologists aren't supposed to equate the behavior and feelings of animals with the behavior and feelings of humans. In science, anthropomorphizing is a cardinal sin. But orca experts like Lance Barrett-Lennard, head of the Vancouver Aquarium's cetacean research program, have stopped avoiding the comparisons, since orca behaviors mimic virtually every trait humans point to as justification for our self-proclaimed perch at the top of the food chain. Says Barrett-Lennard, "We think a young killer whale learns its language, learns what to eat, learns how it's going to interact socially from its kin, from its neighbors, and particularly from its mother. If that's not culture, then I don't know what culture is."

Language? Each pod has its own unique dialect, and it's not innate—it's taught by elders, and their skills continue to develop as they age. The whales also communicate using sophisticated sonar systems that humans still don't understand.

Cooperation? The orcas hunt together strategically and almost never stray from their community.

Compassion? They risk their lives for each other and share their food—no matter how scarce.

No one doubts that orcas are intelligent. The big questions are how smart are they, and what should that mean for our relationships with them? *Saturday Night Live* once created a list of "people dolphins are more intelligent than" and named that era's most famous pop culture punch lines. Although a comedian could still get laughs suggesting dolphins and orcas are more intelligent than a rock star du jour or Republican presidential candidate, maybe the real mystery is whether somewhere in one of our oceans is an orca Einstein. Every bar that's set to prove human superiority to orcas seems to be as easy for the whales to jump as the hurdles set out for them at SeaWorld. Orcas fit every definition for humanity humans have come up with that doesn't require opposable thumbs.

CHAPTER EIGHT

FROM MOBY DICK TO MOBY DOLL

"A killer whale would come as close as anything to being the ultimate aquarium specimen."
CRAIG PHILLIPS, *THE CAPTIVE SEA*, 1963

IMMEDIATELY AFTER MARINELAND'S bid for the captive whale went public, Newman received a second offer from closer to home. Charlie White, operator of Victoria's Undersea Gardens, told anyone who would listen that he would match or beat Marineland's price. When Newman balked, White upped the ante, offering to build a new facility in Vancouver just to house Hound Dog. White claimed he would do what the aquarium couldn't—find the money to build a proper whale tank. Fast. But although everyone seemed impressed by the price tag—which was enough to buy a mansion in Shaughnessy, Vancouver's most exclusive neighborhood—Newman picked another impossibly huge number out of thin air and declared that $20,000 was nothing because the scientific value of his whale was "a million dollars."

Before anyone could balk at the outrageous sum, Dr. Clifford Carl, director of the B.C. Provincial Museum, publicly backed Newman's claim, declaring that the research value of the aquarium's catch was incalculable. "Vancouver's captured killer whale is a living laboratory that could help scientists and medical researchers unravel many mysteries," said Carl. "A relatively recent discovery is that porpoises, and probably all whales, have an echo-sounding device which enables them to locate objects in their path. Recent study has also shown they use a surprisingly small amount of energy in proportion to their speed, and this efficiency is connected in some way with the relatively loose nature of their skin. Experiments indicate that the principle of the flexible covering may be used to great advantage in the designing of faster ships and submarines... Much can be learned by observing it," he concluded, "even in the unnatural surroundings of its present quarters."

Now that they were no longer going to dissect the whale and analyze the pieces—the preferred mode of animal research at the time—scientists made plans to test Hound Dog's heart, brain, bodily fluids, and chromosomes. Blood specialists from the University of Washington arrived to take samples and check the circulation to determine why whales weren't crushed by water pressure. Other researchers puzzled over how to collect a cheek swab from the unpredictable creature to analyze the chromosomes. Scientists were still convinced that if they reached into the whale's mouth to take a sample, the whale was likely to sample their arm.

Vancouver mayor Bill Rathie and four of his aldermen (including Aeneas Bell-Irving, who doubled as the newly appointed chair of the aquarium's board) arrived for a private meeting with the world's only captive killer whale. After playing tourist and snapping a lot of photos, Rathie publicly declared his position—sell the whale. "I don't think City Council will put up $500,000 for a special display tank when visitors only have to take a boat into the Georgia Strait to see a killer whale," Rathie told reporters. "If they can get $20,000 for only five days' work I think the aquarium should maintain a permanent whale-hunting expedition."

The debate was on. Twelve-year-old Debbie Acheson challenged the mayor in a letter to the editor of the *Sun*.

This statement is foolish for several reasons. Not everyone has the money Mayor Rathie has and the average Canadian citizen cannot afford to spend $15 or $30 on renting a boat and motoring to Georgia Strait on chance of seeing a whale. Is Mayor Rathie aware of the fact that if he sells this whale to the States they will probably make a tourist as well as a scientific exhibit out of it and in time have all costs paid for? Does he realize the suffering the whale would go through if it was moved to the States? Is Mayor Rathie aware of the fact that this is only the second killer whale caught alive? Isn't it too good a chance to pass up to the States? Isn't Vancouver supposed to be a tourist city and shouldn't it be looking for big attractions? Can Mayor Rathie not see the scientific value of this creature? Why not give our own Canadian scientists a go at it?

It's a testament to how preoccupied Newman was that Debbie wasn't immediately offered a position as the aquarium's youngest board member.

The convention committee of the Greater Vancouver Tourist Association agreed with Debbie and urged the city to find the funds to keep the whale—both because it would be a great tourist attraction and because it would be such a boon to medical and marine science (since tourist associations are famous supporters of scientific research).

Not everyone was as keen on ponying up to keep the whale, however, and the *Sun* sparked the first blackfish backlash with a front-page story headlined: "Throw Whale Back, Residents Urge." But the story didn't back up the headline or reporter Al Bernie's thesis declaring the city would be better off without the whale. Bernie's unscientific poll of fifty random citizens focused on whether it would be worth a half million dollars to keep the whale. For most people surveyed, the issue wasn't captivity but cost. People seemed to like the idea of keeping the whale—as long as someone else (like Undersea Gardens or the scientists studying it) picked up the tab for what one person referred to as "a fat fish."

Only three people in the story expressed concern for the captive. "Throw it back," said Sharon Breslin. "It would be cruel to keep a big thing like that penned up." A couple of the citizens surveyed worried about the whale's potential victims. "If someone ever fell into the tank and was killed, they'd probably get rid of it anyway," said Irma Parsons. Harold MacIntosh agreed: "They should get rid of it as soon as they can—it's dangerous."

Sun cartoonist Len Norris captured the mood with his drawing of three dignified old businessmen on the edge of the dry dock listening to the whale with a hydrophone. His caption translated the whale's chatter: "See-if-you-can-con-City-Council-for-a-half-million-buck-playpen."

Newman said he'd find the best possible home that would allow scientists to study his specimen, even if that meant sending it to California. Newman knew Marineland had a state-of-the-art tank. But he was hoping the military's makeshift pen would save the whale and the day.

AS THE MEDIA and public pondered the price and value of the whale, McGeer was wondering how to keep it healthy. Despite the gunfire from Burich and the Saturna islanders, on close inspection McGeer found no evidence of bullet wounds. It seemed Burich had been so shaken by the sight of the whale that all of his shots missed their mark—but the cut from the harpoon was festering. McGeer believed that since the whale was a mammal, penicillin would kill any infection, but he had a major mystery on his hands. How do you get a killer whale to take a dose of penicillin, especially when it isn't eating?

In addition to contacting every medical expert in Vancouver, and anyone he could find anywhere who had ever cared for a whale, McGeer recruited veterinarians from the city's racetrack for advice on inoculating large animals. Dr. Joe Lomas, veterinarian for the B.C. Racing Association, told reporters, "As far as we know, nobody in the world ever gave a penicillin shot to a whale before. There's nothing in any of the books about it. We're estimating this whale weighs about 2 ½ tons and we're giving it about twice what we'd give a horse."

The first attempt to give the whale medication was a major feat of engineering.

Since no one in their right mind would touch the monster with a ten-foot pole, McGeer's volunteers assembled a ten-foot pole (some media reported it as twelve feet), attached a four-inch syringe to it, and used it like a spear. "Because we didn't want to lower the water at that time just to administer the antibiotic the idea was to put the plunger at the end of a ten-foot tube and then jam it," says McGeer. "So we just had a large syringe with penicillin in it and a long plunger, the idea being that if it got an infection because of that rope, this would effectively kill it."

CBC TV news reported that "a box containing four men was lowered to the surface of the water, and Dr. Pat McGeer and Vince Penfold, the aquarium's assistant curator, gave the female whale a shot of penicillin... The whale had to be held by a gaff hook on the remains of the harpoon rope. Once the injection was made the rope was cut loose, allowing the animal complete freedom." McGeer's hope was that removing the rope would improve the whale's attitude and appetite. He did not like leaving a foreign object in the injured animal, even if that meant the whale would be more difficult to move.

According to the *Province*, "The restless circling whale got its shots from a massive 12-foot plastic syringe, tipped by a four inch hypodermic needle, pumped into its tough hide by shirt-sleeved McGeer and Gerry Van Easton, UBC zoologist. It took the strength of two men to pierce the hide and four inches of blubber. To get on top of their patient, McGeer and Van Easton were suspended in an ingenious sling dangled above the pen by a 100-foot dry-dock crane. They waited patiently until the circling mammal passed below them, then gave it the works." Van Easton said once the needle pierced the whale's skin, it slid through the blubber like a knife through butter. There were two other passengers in the hanging basket—Penfold and a photographer from *Life*—the world's most popular magazine. Hound Dog was a rising star.

After giving the whale its shot, McGeer shot the whale again— this time with a pistol that was used for tranquilizing wild animals. McGeer fired several darts filled with penicillin and vitamin B-12. Two darts bounced off the whale as if they'd hit Superman's chest. But two appeared to pierce the shiny skin. McGeer declared himself "very satisfied" with the treatment and hopeful about his patient's prospects.

Province reporter Wilf Bennett was less optimistic. "The whale was slightly tilted to one side all the time, apparently finding it difficult to straighten up. It doesn't look well. I don't know what this difficulty with buoyancy means, but I know that every time one of my goldfish gets this tilt, it isn't many days until we find it floating belly up, no longer alive!" The whale's would-be buyers were also watching the patient's progress and reconsidering their sizable offers.

McGeer's major concern was the whale's refusal to eat. Attempts to stuff fish with megadoses of vitamins and suspend them on a rope and wire device designed to make it look like they were alive and swimming repeatedly failed to entice Hound Dog. McGeer was hoping the B-12 would stimulate his patient's appetite. He was also hoping to make the whale an offer it couldn't refuse. Based on stories of whales eating horses, horse hearts were lowered into the pen. The whale was about as excited by the prospect of eating horse hearts as you are.

On July 20, the front-page headline of the *Province* blared: "Our Whale Has Lost Its Appetite." The next day, the whale's diet made the front page again when the *Sun* declared: "Whale Takes a Pint-Sized Meal," after someone was certain they saw Hound Dog gulp a live two-pound flounder. McGeer was not as impressed as reporters were. "It is like a man eating a peanut," he said. "But it is certainly most encouraging."

McGeer and his collection of instant experts weren't sure what the whale wanted to eat and had no clue how long it could survive without food. Newman initially believed his captive could only live for about a week on its own fat, so he went searching for a treat killer whales were known to feast on in the wild—the tongues of baleen whales. The Western Canada Whaling Company agreed to prepare an emergency care package.

After a week, it seemed the only things the whale had ingested were a two-pound flounder and a six-pound lingcod, and there was doubt about whether the whale had eaten the cod or just knocked it off the line when no one was looking.

To prove he was doing everything possible to care for his captive, Newman invited SPCA officials to visit the dry dock, and they pronounced themselves satisfied with the steps being taken and the condition of the whale. While McGeer focused on the whale's wounds—and its appetite—other observers, like Penfold, were more intrigued by its squeaks and squeals. The assistant curator became one of the whale's most constant companions, and after the military recorded Hound Dog with a hydrophone, Penfold was given custody of their gear. The whale's minders were overjoyed when they heard another whale answer their captive's calls. The other killer seemed to be roughly two miles away, near the Lions Gate Bridge—the same spot where Burich and Bauer had last seen their whale's pod-mate. According to mammalogist Dr. Dean Fisher, "The captive became very excited and sent out louder, rapid chatter sounds when it heard the calls from outside." Fisher and others wondered if this was the whale's mate. Were they talking to each other?

Today, we know the visitor was most likely to be the whale's mother, but it's impossible to be sure, because the recordings didn't capture the visitor's distant sounds, just Hound Dog's.

"Her bleatings have been recorded on tape which has been fed into a machine known as a Missilizer. This has an electric needle to interpret the sounds on graphs," explained Fisher, who believed the whale made two types of noises. "She makes a calling sound and a response sound. The calling sound, which is similar to a trumpet, seems to be exploratory, the other is more agitated. The whale seems to be saying, 'I hear you.'" Fisher suspected he was listening to distress signals—an orca SOS. "When the whale calms down and gets back to normal, we'll have a great time listening to the sounds it makes." Fisher hoped that, with enough study, intelligent conversation with the whale might be possible. "Marine mammals have a tremendous potential for creative thought."

John O'Malley of B.C.'s Pacific Naval Laboratory was also convinced the chatter wasn't random: "The whales were definitely communicating: when the one in the inlet called, the other would answer."

Newman started musing about using Hound Dog as a honey trap to capture her mate. Instead of one whale, he could have a pair for his aquarium—a breeding pair.

WHEN HOUND DOG'S eviction date arrived, she was still swimming in the dry dock. Wallace had already postponed one refit job, but as any landlord knows, it's never easy to evict a tenant, especially one that weighs several tons. McGeer says that by introducing the public to the whale, Newman had practically forced Wallace to keep caring for it. Still, Wallace was reassured by the news that the military was doing everything it could to construct a new pen. Wallace agreed that if the army could build the whale a home, he'd deliver the tenant—in his dry dock. Since the dry dock was a floating repair bay, Wallace's men would tow it across the water with the whale still inside. Wallace told reporters, "It was the least we could do for a lady in distress."

The military mission was front-page news in Vancouver. Other front-page stories that week included plans by the Canadian government to institute a national health care program, the race riots in Harlem, the Florida Ku Klux Klan's public burning of a copy of the new U.S. civil rights law, and the torching of "a Madison County Negro Church"—the tenth such church burning in two months. As Mississippi burned, the fate of Vancouver's whale was the biggest news in B.C., and it was popping up in papers throughout North America and around the world. But this wasn't just a story about a whale anymore. The navy assigned a half dozen frogmen to Operation Whale Pen, and their challenges included using underwater saws to repair and remake the existing pier.

"The frogmen showed great concern for the future safety of the whale. They carefully examined the sides of the pen underwater to ensure no nails or jagged ends remained to scratch the whale's body," wrote Fred Allgood in the *Sun*. A tugboat crew helped clear the area of debris and created another problem for the crew. "At one stage, the tug lurched into the side of the jetty and uprooted a pile that is needed to carry the weight of the steel plates, but hasty repairs were made. Another bad moment came when sparks from an acetylene torch being used to cut through a bolt ignited a fire on the dock, but it was quickly extinguished... A problem facing workmen is the rotten condition of the wood on the old jetty. One spectator trod on a soft piece of wood Tuesday evening and his foot slipped through the holes." The army donated wire fencing and other materials. Vancouver businesses donated cargo nets and labor.

Even as they built the pen, everyone knew this special delivery would be a logistical nightmare because there was no way to perfectly line up the dry dock with the new pen. There would be a fifteen-foot gap between the dry dock mouth and the opening of the Jericho enclosure, so in order to keep the whale from escaping, the army volunteers crafted a wire tunnel. In 1964, the comparison people used for the device was the type of chute used to guide cattle—but a more current comparable would be the kind of docking station astronauts used decades later to transfer between space stations and shuttles. As an extra security measure, the tunnel was surrounded by nets, just in case the captive escaped. So after the dry dock was towed across the water—with the whale inside—it would have to line up with a chute that was twenty feet long and seventeen feet wide.

The *Sun* reported that

> every possible escape channel is being explored by the army, which regards the whole operation as a war game to test their resourcefulness. Once the chute, being built by Dominion Bridge Co. Ltd., is in position, the steel net at the bow of the dry dock will be raised, and the whale coaxed into exploring the chute by the seamen. A temporary steel net will be thrown across the entrance while workmen hammer the final steel plates in position. Twelve rolls of steel submarine net were unloaded from the RCN [Royal Canadian Navy] base in Esquimalt. This will form the base of the cage with the steel plate above to keep out floating debris and to muffle the wash from boats. Two rafts constructed for observation pens will have hydrophones to record any conversation.

An eight-man crew of divers worked until midnight each night to construct the pen. "It isn't easy," Private Richard Maliki told reporters. "Have you ever tried swinging a hammer under water?"

The night before the scheduled move, three sides of the pen were fenced in, but the final wall wasn't quite finished, and the whale was set to pass under the Lions Gate Bridge around 2 PM. But Bull Matthews wasn't going to be stopped. "She wasn't just a whale. She was our whale."

Meanwhile, there were concerns that the killer whales were planning a military operation of their own—a jail break. CBC TV reported that "in Nanaimo, it's rumored that an invasion of Vancouver waters by killer whales to rescue the captive at Burrard Drydock could be in the offing. A school, or more properly a pod, of four of these mammals maneuvered in Nanaimo harbor this morning, causing a wave of jitters across whale-land. Sentries with binoculars said that the four consisted of one bull, two cows, and a calf. Old timers in Nanaimo say this is the first time these mammals have been known to go right into the harbor. There are concerns that other whales will attack or attempt a rescue." This sparked the Jericho Yacht Club to declare war. The yacht owners publicly opposed the military operation because of concerns that other killers—and even worse, tourists—might attempt to visit their secluded shore.

While the whales supposedly plotted their rescue, humans planned new attacks on the whales. White told reporters that if he couldn't have Vancouver's whale, he'd catch one himself—and claimed he'd heard of two other groups considering their own hunts. Dr. Carl worried that others trying to capture a killer might not be as lucky as Burich and Bauer. Just because these men survived didn't mean future whalers could expect to escape a tragic fate, and he warned would-be hunters about the *Geronimo*'s debacles. On a more upbeat note, Carl suggested that in time, Vancouver's whale might be trained to do tricks like captive dolphins; he believed these whales could be trained but not trusted. As he told the *Colonist*, "There was one report of a killer whale dumping a crew of men out of a sealing boat, and when they were rescued there was one man missing. He might have drowned but most of the survivors were convinced that he was swallowed."

Newman knew that part of selling the whale to the public was coming up with a better name than "the whale." Burich's nickname, Hound Dog, did not catch on with the media, who'd taken to calling his prize "the whale," "our whale," or "Vancouver's whale." Hound Dog also didn't seem like the proper name for a potentially pregnant female. The *Sun* reported that "since it was discovered that the whale is female, a more glamorous name is being sought." The media suggested headline-worthy monikers such as Calamity Jane and Jericho Jenny.

Ten-year-old Wanda Robinson raised two dollars to help house the whale and shared her story in a letter to the editor of the *Sun*: "We read in the paper that the mayor wants to sell the whale that was caught last week. Yesterday myself and the kids on our street held a carnival in our basement and raised $2. We would like to donate this money to whoever is in charge of the whale in the hopes it may help keep it in Vancouver. We would also like to suggest the name of

Bo-Peep for our whale." The letter listed the names of her fellow fin fans, aged six to eleven. Wanda—who shared her name with the first ever captive killer—wanted to call the whale Bo-Peep because of the way it squeaked.

On July 22, CBC TV reported that "a *Life* magazine photographer was on hand to record the antics of the killer whale while a woman reporter from *Life* was also there to write the saga of the whale." The broadcaster also revealed the whale's new name. So did reporter Fred Allgood, who wrote that the whale was christened "by Vancouver's Captain Ahab—Dr. Murray Newman."

The name: Moby Doll.

CHAPTER NINE

MILLION-DOLLAR BABY

"Then came Moby's finest hour. She refused to cooperate, backed, turned, attacked the boat and fought for
her freedom. For 20 minutes she glared angrily at the
crowd around the pen and flicked her tail defiantly."
FRED ALLGOOD, *VANCOUVER SUN*, JULY 25, 1964

I N HIS AUTOBIOGRAPHY, Newman wrote, "Celebrity fishes are
great for free publicity, and it is an unwise aquarist who forgets
or disdains the fact that one of the first aquarium directors was
P.T. Barnum." Newman was sharing the story of his first undersea
celebrity—a "mystery fish" his staff couldn't identify that briefly captivated the Canadian media in 1956, but he could easily have been
writing about the whale he'd named Moby Doll.

Moby Doll was moving to a new home, and the world was watching. Reporters, photographers, and filmmakers hitched a lift on the
dry dock to chronicle the whale's wild ride. Burich, Penfold, and Wallace's crew rode shotgun. Bauer waited at Jericho to watch the divers
finish their job. And Moby was on the strangest trip any whale had
ever taken—trapped in a moving pen surrounded by the relentless
sounds of the people, towboats, a moving dry dock, and every other
ship in the crowded harbor.

The day of the move, the *Province* reporter who'd worried that
Moby was listing wrote that the whale "appeared livelier... It swam

83

faster, straighter and spouted higher." Wilf Bennett reported what he'd been told—that the reason the whale tilted wasn't because of illness but curiosity. She was watching the scientists, and the position of the whale's eyes meant the only way to get a clear view was to lean.

"She was definitely giving us the eye," McGeer told him.

The *Province* also reminded readers that Canadians used to love their whales... for lunch. The paper reported that cans of diced whale loin used to be available "with added gravy" in local supermarkets for ten cents. The label on the seventeen-ounce can promised a mix of "whale meat, meat gravy, onion, celery salt, black pepper, cayenne pepper and salt." Each tin included instructions for three recipes— meat pie, curried whale, and whale stew. The story concluded, "It didn't go over well with Vancouver housewives and has long since disappeared from grocers' shelves. But in Japan, whale—which is mammal—is bought by the ton and cooked in many a kitchen." Yes, Moby Doll might be special but not that special.

A newspaper ad for insurance adjusters rode the Moby wave. Their pitch referred to their employees as intelligent mammals and urged potential clients to "depend on insurance, not a fluke."

Meanwhile, B.C. premier W.A.C. Bennett acknowledged Moby while boasting to reporters about his plans to launch a provincial bank. Bennett joked that "Vancouver already has a whale, BC will have a whale of a bank as well."

Perhaps because *Life* had commissioned a special cage that would protect their underwater photographer so that he could shoot close-ups of the captive, Penfold began hedging his bets on the whale's gender, backing away from his pronouncement that Moby was female and suggesting that it was possible she was a he. This prompted reporters to speculate that Moby Doll might be Moby Dick or should at least be referred to as "Moby Maybe." Penfold said he'd hold off on a definitive answer until he could get a closer look at the captive.

A few days later, Penfold made the announcement everyone was waiting for. "It's a girl." Penfold, who was a diver, went into the cage with the *Life* photographer, took a look at Moby's underside, and reported that he could confirm the whale's sex. Even as Penfold publicly declared that Moby was a female, Newman wasn't completely convinced. But Bauer says Penfold was. "He told me I was totally dead wrong about it being a male."

As Moby Doll swam in her usual counterclockwise pattern, the media, researchers, dockworkers, and VIPs (including representatives from Marineland and Canada's fisheries minister) gathered to send the whale on her way. McGeer shared the good news that the whale's wounds were healing. But she still wasn't eating. Three salmon had vanished, but Newman and McGeer suspected she was playing with her food, not swallowing it.

Marineland's curator informed Newman of another potential problem—stress. If the whale didn't calm down, it could get an ulcer. After hearing this news, McGeer considered adding tranquilizers to the whale's mix of medications, but Newman could have used them too. In an apparent attempt to give Newman an ulcer, Marineland's general manager denied that he'd offered $20,000 for Moby but said that if the whale lived a month, it would be very valuable. He wasn't prepared to say how valuable, and Newman stood by his claim that they'd offered $20,000. Newman's biggest worry was that the complicated moving operation wouldn't work.

Preparations for towing started at 8:45 AM, and the journey began at 9:45 so that the tide could help propel the dry dock across the water. The dockworkers waved good-bye to their guest, and the whale flicked her tail and blew spray at the start of her send-off. "Hauled into Burrard Drydock a week ago, harpooned, hurt and humiliated, Moby left in high style," wrote the *Sun's* Ian MacDonald. "A fleet of small tugs pulled and fussed around the water-filled dock, while inside Moby swam lazily in circles."

The pen traveled the seven miles across the water at between three and four knots. Perhaps because it was a military operation, the trip began with military precision, and the fleet of a half dozen tugs was accompanied by a naval vessel. Meanwhile, navy divers raced to finish their cage before the convoy arrived. Whale watchers crowded the shoreline, approached by boat, and someone even flew over the dry dock in a floatplane to witness the epic journey.

It was all smooth sailing, until a ferry sent ripples through the water. The *Sun* reported that ten-foot-high waves "rocked the dry-dock and caused Moby Doll to squeal in panic as the water heaved violently. Three of the five lines holding an accompanying powered scow snapped." Fortunately, Wallace had sent fifteen men to super-vise the move. The workers quickly reconnected the lines. In about ten minutes, the waves, whale, and moving men had calmed down.

Once the dry dock arrived at the naval base, the moving team had to wait four hours for the water to rise so that they could take advan-tage of the 4:20 flood tide. This extra time allowed navy divers to take one last tour of the pen to confirm that it wasn't just closed off from outside waters but also clear of debris and sharp edges. The *Life* photographer and a CBC cameraman tried to take underwater photos of the whale inside the dry dock, but the water wasn't clear enough.

When the foreman felt the tide and time were right for the trans-fer, he signaled the tugs and ordered his crew to hook up the chute. Once everything was set and the tide lifted the rear of the dry dock, the perfect plan fell apart. Fred Allgood from the *Sun* referred to what happened next as "Moby's finest hour."

The *Colonist* described it as "a stubborn cat-and-mouse battle with her captors."

The *Toronto Star* called it "the most bizarre moving day Vancouver has ever seen."

The whale had arrived at her new home, but she wasn't moving.

"Moby lost her self-control and gave a display of feminine temper," wrote Allgood. "She squirmed in the water, thrashed angrily, twisted in many directions and howled into the hydrophone Dr. McGeer had concealed in the dock."

The dry dock was lowered by a pump, the back end was raised, and Moby was expected to float down the chute and into her new home. Burich and Penfold hopped into a small boat to guide their whale, but she wasn't interested. "She refused to cooperate, backed, turned, attacked the boat and fought for her freedom. For 20 minutes she glared angrily at the crowd around the pen and flicked her tail defiantly," wrote Allgood.

The *Province* reported that "the captured killer whale bucked, twisted, squealed angrily, thrashed the water and charged the boat that tried to nudge her into her new home."

That was when Penfold probably became the first human in history to intentionally hit a whale. After two hours of trying to cajole, dump, and scare the captive into her new home, the no-nonsense former prison guard grabbed the whale's dorsal fin and shoved it in an attempt to shock her into moving. The crowd of scientists, frogmen, army engineers, dockworkers, and media cheered. Moby Doll was unfazed. She didn't snap at Penfold, but she didn't change direction either.

Allgood reported that was when "Dr. Newman decided that there was too much noise on the jetty and suggested it should be cleared. Col. Matthews took his cue, barked out a crisp order to clear the jetty and in a few minutes single-handedly herded the entire crowd away... Navy men were ordered off the decks of the tenders alongside the pier and the engineers at the pen entrance huddled close to the wooden floor. An eerie silence descended on the dock."

Newman was impressed. With just the power of his voice, Bull Matthews had cleared the docks of everyone except *Sun* photographer Deni Eagland, who watched everything from his perch on a forty-four-foot ladder. Then Newman called the cops and asked them to turn on their boat's siren to scare the whale. The sound must have been excruciating to Moby's acute acoustic senses.

"With Penfold and Burich prodding with their paddles, the net dragging and police siren blaring, the whale was hustled to the lip of the pen," wrote Allgood. "Three times she ducked away, and once found herself stranded on the bottom of the dry dock. With a heave and a twist she refloated herself. The fire had gone out of her and she slipped into the pen defeated. Engineers quickly lowered the gate in position. Moby Doll was home…. No mighty bull killer whales greeted her distress signals, and so she surrendered suddenly, and reluctantly drifted into her new pen at Jericho. She sensed she was trapped. Instead of charging the army engineers as they bolted the gate of her new pen in position, she meekly circled her new home."

It was just after 7 PM, and once again, the whale's timing was perfect. With minutes to spare, Moby made it to air as one of the top stories on the evening news. After almost ten hours, the adventure was over. Two aldermen were on hand to give the whale and its entourage an official civic welcome. SPCA observers told reporters they had no complaints about what they had witnessed.

The *Sun* declared, "It was a climax to nine days of adventure, courage, ingenuity and teamwork by the army, navy, Vancouver Aquarium, University of B.C. scientists, Burrard Dry Dock, tug boat companies, department of national defense, department of fisheries, private companies and police."

It turned out that Wallace hadn't just been a gracious host but also a generous one. In addition to the dry dock, he'd provided an auxiliary power barge and the fifteen men who worked fifteen-hour shifts to move Moby.

When it was all over and Newman no longer had to sound optimistic and inspirational, he confessed his fears to reporters as he surveyed the scene. "Wow, I wasn't really sure she was going to make it." Newman also explained what he suspected was the cause of Moby's reticence to enter the chute connecting the dry dock to the pen. "This is a very intelligent animal. It has a type of built-in radar and emits supersonic sounds, so that it knew all the time we were trying to force it through a funnel." Exhausted, Newman called it a day and went home to rest.

Exhilarated, McGeer climbed into the empty dry dock to look for fish and lost medical instruments. He discovered the remains of all the fish Moby was believed to have eaten—except for two flounders. He also found lost syringes and some of the pellets full of medicine he'd believed had penetrated the whale's skin. Moby had received almost none of the medication McGeer had provided. But McGeer refused to be discouraged. He told reporters it was possible that the noisy dry dock had put Moby off her food and that this new, quieter home would allow her to finally recover from the shock of being harpooned and adjust to her new life with humans.

Before the move, Newman had claimed his whale was worth a million dollars. After the move, the media was forced to accept his appraisal.

On July 25, the front-page headline of the *Province* blared: "Our Whale's a Million Dollar Baby." The story described the previous day's adventure as a "$1 million moving and storage job." Their math: "Officials estimate it would have cost them about this much to care for Moby Doll during the past week, prepare her new home and move her there in a $500,000 dry-dock—if the bills had to be paid." The *Toronto Star* agreed with this estimate. "Counting the equipment and the man hours of about 100 toilers it all amounted to a million dollar effort." Vancouver City Council sent thank-you notes to everyone who helped move the whale.

The expensive move didn't just create a temporary home for Moby but also gave Newman the ammunition he needed to finally, definitively announce that his whale was not for sale. After all the time, energy, emotion, and money that had gone into moving Moby, Newman declared it wouldn't be fair to the city to sell her. Moby Doll was Vancouver's whale.

A FEW DAYS after being quoted that he was signing off on Moby Doll's pen at Jericho, an SPCA representative wrote a letter that ran in the *Sun* and the *Province* clarifying that his group was opposed to Moby's capture but not the whale's current conditions. "Let there be no misunderstanding. The SPCA has condemned and will continue to condemn the capture of a killer whale. The whole episode was shamefully inhumane in concept and conduct. The SPCA on Sunday attempted to allay public concern over its condition as we found it. The SPCA statement was not fully reported. In our final paragraph we said, 'Meanwhile, SPCA officials will continue their investigations into all circumstances of its capture.'" However, in a CBC TV interview with SPCA officials, it appeared they were under the impression that catching a live whale was intentional.

In late August, in a letter to the *Sun*, the SPCA petitioned for Moby's release: "Now that Moby Doll has been declared recovered from the harpoon wound and therefore able to fend for herself, she should be set free forthwith. The SPCA has condemned its capture as shamefully inhumane in concept and conduct. Its continued incarceration is a disgrace. The grandiose plans for a permanent prison are without moral or financial justification... How much longer must this animal suffer, at mounting public expense, for the amusement of experts engaged in dubious experiments which so far have added nothing to an already extensive knowledge of killer whales?"

The SPCA followed up by protesting news that the aquarium was feeding Moby live fish—a complaint that was ridiculed in a *Sun* editorial.

> Just what would the SPCA expect Moby Doll to eat if she were set free? Dead or painlessly killed fish? Found where? Provided by whom? The two protests taken together hardly make sense. A good deal of meaningless sentimentality has been wasted on Moby Doll. The killer whale goes by several other names. One of them is "the tiger of the seas." It is probably one of the most ferocious and destructive animals in the world... The capture and retention of Moby Doll is a unique opportunity for the scientific study of this awesome engine of destruction. And so far as live codfish go, it is more than likely that on Fridays many SPCA members dine on codfish caught on a long line, brought to market in a live box and slaughtered for their benefit. Does it make any difference to the cod whether it ends up inside Moby Doll or inside a member of the SPCA?

McGeer warned that releasing the awesome engine of destruction could be fatal to it, because whales hunt with their families and there was no way to reunite it with its pod. SPCA officials later deferred to McGeer and backed off on their calls to release the whale.

One person who was unequivocally appalled by the capture was seventy-six-year-old Maisie Hurley, who issued dire prophecies that if the whale weren't freed "not only will disaster befall Vancouver, but the whale will die."

Several stories about Hurley's predictions portrayed her as a wacky crackpot, but they neglected to mention her lifelong work on behalf of B.C.'s First Nations. Born in Wales in 1887, with ties to the British aristocracy, Hurley had arrived in Canada at age three. Despite her overseas origins, Hurley became the first female member of the Native Brotherhood of B.C. in 1944. Two years later, she launched the *Native Voice*—Canada's first First Nations newspaper—with her own money. Hurley also knew how to grab a headline. When she wasn't fighting for social justice, she worked as a boxing manager and promoter.

In 1949, Gitxsan chief Arthur McDanes honored Hurley with the name Chief SimKlaus, which translated as "Mother of the Finback Whales." In an interview with the *Sun*, the Mother of the Finbacks (another name for killer whales) shared a legend to explain why orcas were never hunted.

> Once upon a time, about 70 years ago, an Indian princess named Lucy died... All the Indians mourned and wept and Lucy's husband, Supple Jack, ordered that the body not be buried but placed beside the sea for three days because Lucy had been a member of the Order of the Finback Whales... So Lucy's body was laid out on the beach and in the night, when all the tribe were asleep, the finback whales took it away below the waters of the First Narrows... They took Lucy to see the King of the Fin-Back Whales, he looked at her and decided that she should live. So he ordered the whales to take her back to shore alive.

The whales obeyed orders, and the next morning Supple Jack found his wife alive—but sleepy—on the beach. "Lucy kept saying how tired she was and then she told all the Indians about her adventures under the sea... Naturally, after that, the Indians have always been very grateful to the whales and the legend grew up that it would be disastrous for anyone to harm a fin-back." Hurley told the *Sun* that Lucy lived for many years after her encounter with the finback and that one of her children was Chief August Jack Khatsahlano.

What the story didn't mention was that Hurley was friends with Khatsahlano. The two used to prospect for gold together, and Khatsahlano not only attended Hurley's wedding but blessed the bride and groom. When Hurley spoke on behalf of First Nations, she was never just speaking for herself, she was speaking for friends like Chief Khatsahlano.

The story ended on a glib note by interviewing Haida artist Bill Reid, who was identified as "another local Indian expert." Reid said he wasn't too concerned about Hurley's prophecies. "We're probably having the disaster right now," quipped Reid. "All this rain."

Gordon Pike was also quoted as saying in a speech that Moby should be set free. The local whale expert almost immediately claimed that he had been quoted out of context and clarified his position. "Emotionally, you don't like to see an animal as intelligent as the whale penned up. But weighing this against science she absolutely should not be released."

The most surprising and passionate complaints about keeping Moby in captivity came from an unofficial member of the original hunting party, *Sun* reporter Jack Scott.

That I happen to be one of those who favor her release and believe that most British Columbians would rejoice in the act of granting her freedom may seem at odds with the fact that I was with the original party at the East Point Light which had the sole purpose of destroying a specimen. I rationalize that though I'm not at all sure that I'm right, in much the same manner that I rationalize experimental vivisection. The specific aim was a reasonable one, to use the carcass for the construction of an accurate model which would be edifying to the large numbers of visitors to the Vancouver Public Aquarium and possibly to add to the scant scientific knowledge of an animal that rarely falls victim to man... Just as there can be abuses of vivisection, I now feel, in the light of the miracle of taking Moby Doll alive, that this operation, organized with the best of intentions by Dr. Murray Newman, is in danger of turning sour...

At no risk of sentimentally humanizing the one creature least likely to be tamed by man, it can be said that this killer whale has endured the gamut of pain, fear, humiliation and intolerable confinement. Thus, it would seem only common justice that she now be given the one meaningful reward we can grant. To carry through the plan of making her a sort of side-show freak, permanently incarcerated in a prison where she's more likely to be a subject of pity than anything else is, to use the words of the SPCA, "without moral or financial justification."

Scott's column concluded: "Like certain land animals, notably the tiger and mountain lion, this monarch of the sea may serve only as a symbol of man's sometimes sadistic impulses to conquer and crush the spirit of other creatures who share occupation on this soil. To do that merely for the amusement of spectators is hardly a valid reason for continued captivity. I hope they will release her. I would like to be there when that great black fin heads for deep blue water, if only to ease my own troubled conscience."

The first killer whale in captivity had launched the first anti-captivity activists.

The controversy didn't keep anyone away from the aquarium. Even though the whale was never on display there, the aquarium set box office records that July, drawing 82,000 people, topping their previous monthly attendance record by 10,000.

The protests that were a bigger issue for Newman had nothing to do with captivity and everything to do with the phenomenon known as NIMBY—not in my back yard. Newman and McGeer knew their whale couldn't stay at Jericho. Not only was the water too dirty to allow researchers—or paying customers—to get a good look at Moby, but the scientists worried that the lack of salinity might harm their specimen. Even if they could find a way to make viewing viable and the water whale friendly, the yacht club didn't want visiting killer whales potentially snacking on sailboats, nevermind riffraff cruising for parking spots.

Newman found four viable homes for Moby—and his aquarium wasn't one of them. Even if he could finish his proposed dolphin pool in record time, Newman thought it was too small to comfortably house a whale, and the Parks Board was concerned that an expansion of the aquarium would disturb the duck pond—and, apparently, they loved that duck pond. The proposal for a solution that would work financially and logistically was to build an enclosure like the one at Jericho but adjacent to the open ocean and out of the harbor so that Moby could be displayed in as natural an environment as possible.

A pitch to move to the seaside off one suburban park was quickly dismissed with the response possibly best summed up in an angry letter complaining that humans needed a new public swimming pool before the money was found to house "an expensive hunk of blubber." Even fans of the whale weren't fans of paying to care for it.

The most promising potential home was off the shore of the affluent suburb of West Vancouver. Its municipal council members were excited by the idea of playing host to the cetacean superstar, but the community's well-heeled voters didn't want tourists crowding their streets or stealing their picnic spots. The most vocal complaints about building a permanent seaside pen weren't about having a whale in captivity but about having a whale as a neighbor.

CHAPTER TEN

THE ULTIMATE EXHIBIT

"The Museum having expended altogether a sum not much less than $17,000 in the whaling business, this is probably the last attempt that will be made to exhibit a living whale in connection with the other expensive attractions of the Museum for only twenty-five cents. With these remarks, I leave this monster leviathan to do his own spouting, not doubting that the public will embrace the earliest moment (before it is forever too late) to witness the most novel and extraordinary exhibition ever offered them in this City."

P.T. BARNUM, 1861

A S MOBY DOLL swam in slow counterclockwise circles around her Jericho pen, Newman began picturing the whale doing tricks that would dazzle his customers. The pilot whales at Marineland knew how to shake hands, wave, and dance for the crowds—and killers were smarter than pilots.

The first whales that made a real splash with the North American public were courtesy of America's legendary showman Phineas Taylor Barnum. In 1861, Barnum heard that fishermen had captured a live beluga in Canada's St. Lawrence River. He was smitten with the idea of owning his own great white whale and built a forty-by-eighteen-foot tank in the basement of his New York museum. After constructing his aquarium, Barnum went to the St. Lawrence and recruited two dozen fishermen to trap a pair of whales. He was determined to display a duo.

Once Barnum had his whales, he spread the word that his new star exhibits would be traveling by train to New York so that crowds would gather to watch them on their journey. But instead of transporting the whales in a tank of salt water, Barnum's crew put them in salted freshwater. Barnum's belugas were a smash with the public, and thousands of people saw them—before they drowned less than forty-eight hours after being placed on display. Convinced that his "leviathans" had the potential to be a jumbo hit (like his famous elephant, Jumbo), Barnum ordered the construction of a new tank on the second floor of his museum. He also hired workers to build a pipe to New York Bay and hook it up to a steam engine so that his new whales could swim in proper seawater.

But his second pair of whales died in transit, before getting a chance to test the new tank.

Despite the $17,000 Barnum spent on "the whaling business"—a sum that could have bought him his own whaling fleet—the deaths weren't enough to convince him to abandon belugas. "A real live whale is as great a curiosity as a live lord or prince, being much more difficult to catch, and far more wonderful in its appearance and habits," according to a piece in the New-York Tribune that may have been penned by a Barnum press agent or Barnum himself. "After all people are people, and have much the same ways of feeling and doing. But when we get among the whales, we catch glimpses of a new and neat thing in nose, recall the narrative of Jonah without throwing a shadow of a doubt upon its authenticity, and appreciate keenly the difficulties with which mermaid society must have to contend."

Barnum displayed several other belugas at his New York Aquarium—and at the Boston Aquarial Gardens (which he renamed Barnum's Aquarial Gardens). None of them survived for long. In 1865, Barnum brought two new belugas to New York. They were also a hit and appeared to be thriving—until his museum caught fire. In an attempt to douse the blaze, employees smashed the whale tank to let the water out. The *New York Times* reported that "the whales were, of course, burned alive. At an early stage of the conflagration, the large panes of glass in the great 'whale tank' were broken to allow the heavy mass of water to flow upon the floor of the main saloon, and the leviathan natives of Labrador, when last seen, were floundering in mortal agony." The museum was destroyed. The whales rotted in public, on America's most famous street. Their legacy: biggest stench in Broadway history.

Moby Doll confirmed that Barnum was right. The world was fascinated by leviathans.

AFTER MOBY MOVED into her new home, the man who had harpooned the monster and then shot at it three times became the world's first killer whale–sitter. Burich began hovering over the whale like an anxious parent from the day he led his catch into the dry dock. "Killer whales aren't used to being alone," Burich told reporters. "I wanted her to know she had a friend." Bauer joined Burich whenever possible, taking photos of the whale he'd spotted and joking with Burich. The men who'd spent two months keeping watch for a whale to kill now kept watch over a killer whale.

Burich showed up at Jericho every morning at six and stayed until after dark. Since whales seemed to communicate with squeaks, he thought he could try speaking her language—or at least create similar noises to show that he was making an effort to talk back to her. When Moby surfaced, he'd whistle a tune or play his harmonica, hoping his sounds might connect with the creature. "Sometimes she seems to squeal in response," Burich told reporters, "but maybe it's just my imagination."

For the first three days at Jericho, Burich stayed a safe distance away from his charge, on top of the wharf, watching as the whale surfaced every minute or so. Then he started sitting at the edge of the pen, eventually doing something that would have terrified him a few weeks earlier—dangling his legs over the side of the dock, risking the possibility of becoming another Ahab complete with a peg leg. He still didn't trust killer whales, but he trusted Moby Doll.

It wasn't long before Burich began sitting on a canvas chair on a six-by-six-foot raft that Moby could have easily smashed. But he wanted to get as close as possible to his model. Moby swam under his raft a few times but mostly steered clear. "I am running out of new ideas on how to get her to trust me," Burich admitted. Sometimes he'd get on his hands and knees to get closer to the water. After deciding that his harmonica didn't interest the whale, Burich tried a police whistle. "I think she mimicked the police whistle a few times— maybe it was my imagination. Maybe I was mimicking her when I blew on it."

Back on Saturna, Scott described Burich as "far and away the most dedicated and optimistic of any of us." Burich showed the same dedication and optimism as a whale-sitter that he had as a whale hunter. It was his job to get the whale to eat, and he was determined to succeed. One afternoon, as he tried tempting Moby with fresh salmon, a CBC TV reporter asked Burich about his hopes for her. "Now that she's come so far, I'd like to see her live," he told the CBC. "We'll just have to go out and get another one for a model."

When Burich wasn't guarding the whale, he was spelled off by the B.C. Corps of Commissionaires—retired military men determined to keep anyone from disturbing their guest. The whale was under constant guard.

Penfold also spent as much time as possible at Jericho—always dressed in his white lab coat, always holding a clipboard. Penfold wasn't a scientist, but he played one on TV, often taking the lead in interviews about Moby. He told reporters that he hoped his recordings would lead to discovering evidence of a language. He also let Moby listen to her own calls to see how she responded.

Every time Moby made a new noise, McGeer and Penfold were thrilled. Their plan was to compile a "whale dictionary" in the hope that even if people couldn't communicate with her, they'd be able to understand her. After all, they were now the leading authorities on killer whale talk. William Schevill, the Harvard scientist considered the world's expert on whale sounds, had never heard a killer whale. But he was determined to change that, so he booked a flight to Vancouver.

NEWMAN DIDN'T WANT the public meeting Moby Doll at Jericho. He didn't think it was healthy for the whale, the people, or his aquarium. The water wasn't clear enough to view the whale underwater and the pier wasn't built to accommodate civilians—broken planks might not upset army officers, but parents wouldn't be thrilled if little Johnny or Janie suddenly fell through the brittle wood into the water. The next time Moby was displayed, Newman was determined it would be done properly. His plan was to present the world with a whale that wasn't just healthy but healthy enough to perform.

Other mammals could be fed by hand—surely Moby could be too. It would be like feeding a lion or tiger. Thrilling. Death defying. Hand-feeding the whale was Newman's dream, but starving her was his nightmare. He and his crew tried offering her anything they'd ever heard of whales eating. Moby's menu was regularly reported to the media. On July 27, newspapers announced that Moby had turned up her nose at fifteen flounders, two salmon, three horse hearts, and a lingcod pumped full of oxygen so that it would float like a live fish.

Newman hoped he could break Moby's fast with an offer of fresh whale tongue—courtesy of the whaling station—along with fresh whale meat marinated in blood. Moby was not interested. The aquarium staff also offered up a dead octopus, which also failed to entice the whale. Then UBC zoology student Michael Bigg was recruited to deliver a dead seal and seal blood—two more meals that Moby passed on. Bigg was studying harbor seals, but he found Moby intriguing and became one of the other volunteers regularly monitoring her sounds. While Penfold listened for language, Bigg listened for breathing patterns and did spectrogram recordings to study Moby's respiratory cycle.

There was talk of force-feeding Moby. Marineland's crew told Newman they'd fed pilot whales by prying their mouths open with tongs and throwing in fish. But Newman was worried that Moby's mouthful of flesh-tearing teeth could do a lot more damage than a pilot whale's. He also believed Burich was gaining Moby's trust and was concerned that manhandling the whale would ruin the bond the pair were building. Then a researcher at the Philadelphia Aquarium reassured Newman and McGeer that captive pilots had gone up to two months without eating and convinced them that although Moby might be hungry, she wasn't starving.

Another regular visitor to the whale pen was Aeneas Bell-Irving. The alderman and aquarium president showed up to watch Moby and discreetly put up his own money to commission an architect to design a proper home for her. Bell-Irving agreed that this wasn't the time or place for the public to meet Moby and told reporters that "in a few months, perhaps six, she might be eating out of our hands. That will be worth showing to people." He described the Jericho site as a sick bay or perhaps a maternity bay.

Requests to leave the whale alone to regain her health didn't stop gawkers from trying to sneak a peek. People tried to climb the fences and approached the perimeter on everything from pleasure boats to air mattresses. They were all escorted away by the commissionaires. To relieve the commissionaires—and avoid the cost of twenty-four-hour guards—a six-foot barbed wire fence was strung around the pen. The papers reported that there was now only a single entrance, and Newman had the only key. Since Burich was there every morning, another aquarium worker, Terry McLeod, was there almost every night, and Newman had an aquarium to run, it was an unlikely story—but it did its job. The army also set up a log boom to protect the pen from floating debris.

After a few days at Jericho, Moby was starting to recognize Burich and began responding to his whistles. According to the *Sun*, Moby Doll "forgot she was a lady" and whistled back at her keeper. On August 4, the *Sun* reported that Moby's rapport with Burich was building and that she was swimming closer to him every day. "She only comes when I'm alone," said Burich. "She seems suspicious of others." The whale was adapting to life in captivity, but she still wasn't eating, and when most humans came to visit, she kept to the far side of the pool. McGeer mused that perhaps killer whales weren't as friendly as other dolphins.

Since Moby was responding to Burich's whistles—and soon to Penfold's as well—Newman and McGeer wondered how she'd respond to actual whale whistles and played them to her through the hydrophone speakers to monitor her reactions. McGeer joined Burich on the raft to see how Moby responded to tapes of other whales. "Whatever the wild whales are saying, Moby Doll doesn't like it," McGeer told reporters. "Every time she gets their message she speeds to the far end of the pool. I'd like to know what they say."

Moby was at her chattiest when a pair of whales was spotted under the Lions Gate Bridge. Was one of them Moby's mother? Was one of them Granny? When the other whales were nearby, Moby didn't stop making sounds, but there was no response from the pod.

Although McGeer was intrigued by the idea of communicating with whales, he disapproved of the motives of most of the people trying to make contact with them. Cold Warriors were experimenting with dolphins as weapons. One idea was to turn the creatures into suicide bombers. When *Province* newspaper columnist Himie Koshevoy asked about Moby's military potential, McGeer sarcastically replied, "Just imagine, we could tell them to hunt out enemy subs. Think of North America being ringed by pods of whales on defense for us. They could alert us where and when our enemy would attack. But the Russians might also discover the whales' code. After that we'd have Marxian whales and Democratic whales and the fight would be to win the uncommitted whales of the world to our side."

As Moby's fast continued, Newman wondered if the whale might be eating fish that were swimming into the pen. Finally, Newman and McGeer decided they needed a closer look at their patient. Even if they weren't going to force feed her, they had to administer more medicine and run tests. This time they trapped Moby with a net.

She thrashed around for a few moments but relaxed after McGeer gave her a tranquilizer. He also gave Moby five doses of vitamin B-12, three doses of B-1 to increase appetite, and 12 million units of penicillin in case the harpoon injury was still an issue. McGeer liked the look of the wound—it appeared to be healing—and took blood samples by pressing a syringe into the blubber near the dorsal fin. He was thrilled by how easy it was to collect his samples. He hoped the next time they subdued her, they could take her temperature and run an electrocardiogram to study her heart.

The blood was analyzed to check for infection, run a pregnancy test, and determine what a whale's blood was like. The pathologist found no sign of infection or anemia, the pregnancy test was inconclusive, and the blood was similar to human blood but saltier.

As the doctors gave Moby a clean bill of health, Newman announced a cheaper alternative to the half-million-dollar pen he'd originally proposed and revealed the design Bell-Irving had commissioned. Instead of a new tank on land, they'd build something adjacent to the ocean with underwater glass viewing panels and a lab for researchers. Newman had found four suitable locations, and because Moby would be able to swim in the ocean, no filters or pumps would be required. The outdoor location would allow more large fish—including sharks, dolphins, porpoises, and perhaps other types of whales—to be exhibited.

Since no one knew when or how whales slept, Newman also decided to check Moby's nocturnal habits. Because of several incidents in which sleeping sperm whales had been hit by boats during the day, some scientists theorized that was when whales slept. One night, Newman surprised Moby with a flashlight and immediately got her attention. "She shot straight towards the light until she was underneath it," said Newman. "She seemed lively and responsive and cooperated better than ever before." Moby not only whistled at Newman but also broke from her swimming pattern and began zigzagging and diving. It seemed Newman had finally made friends with Moby.

The next day, Bell-Irving was sure he saw her eat a live fish. After he shared this news, everyone wanted to believe it so much that they became convinced that Bell-Irving was right—even though no one else had spotted the whale eating. Newman mused that perhaps killer whales also ate the way baleen whales such as humpbacks did— skimming plankton from the water. Since Moby was apparently eating, Newman told Burich it was time to start on his sculpture. Although the original plans had been to catch and sculpt a much larger whale, Newman told reporters that his display had to feature Moby. "We'll never get another whale as famous as Moby Doll has become, so we're going to immortalize her."

Burich didn't have the precise measurements or photos that were supposed to inform his work, but the scientists had managed a measurement when Moby was getting her shots. Her length was recorded at fifteen feet and one inch.

On August 14, Burich was relieved of his duties as whale-sitter, but he wasn't leaving. Even though it was no longer his job, Burich was determined to keep visiting Moby, sitting with her, whistling to her, and playing music for her as often as possible—and it had nothing to do with creating an accurate replica. "I'll stay here and help her until she dies at my feet," said Burich. "You become attached to the darn thing."

Setting up the Norwegian harpoon gun on Saturna Island to shoot the first killer whale who swims close enough to shore. Thar she blows... PHOTO BY JOE BAUER.

Sculptor-turned-whaler Sam Burich, longtime aquarium volunteer and collector Joe Bauer, and assistant curator Vince Penfold on Saturna Island preparing for their great whale hunt. June 1964. PHOTO COURTESY OF JOE BAUER.

When the "monster" arrived in Vancouver, the harpoon was still attached to help control the fierce killer whale. PHOTO BY DON MCLEOD, COURTESY OF TERRY MCLEOD.

It seemed like everyone with a camera was taking photos of Moby Doll—including the Vancouver Aquarium's founding curator and the head of the whale-hunting expedition, Murray Newman.

PHOTOS BY MURRAY NEWMAN.

Sculptor and designated harpoonist Sam Burich chiseled his own orca into the sandstone on Saturna while waiting for the killer whales to arrive.

PHOTO BY JOE BAUER.

"It says . . . 'See . . . if . . . you . . . . can . . . con . . . city council . . . for . . . a half-million . . . buck . . . playpen . . . '"

How much is a whale worth? *Vancouver Sun* cartoonist Len Norris breaches the debate over the plans to build a new tank to house Vancouver's biggest celebrity.

JULY 22, 1964. CARTOON COURTESY OF STEPHEN NORRIS.

"The most bizarre moving day Vancouver has ever seen" (*Toronto Star*)—the epic mission to transport the killer whale across Vancouver harbor to the new pen built by military volunteers. PHOTO BY DON MCLEOD, COURTESY OF TERRY MCLEOD.

The media, the military, scientists, and politicians watch Moby Doll maneuver in the new pen. PHOTO BY DON MCLEOD, COURTESY OF TERRY MCLEOD.

As soon as orcas were displayed in marine parks in 1965, every whale show featured feeding time. Terry McLeod was one of the first humans to hand-feed a killer whale, after he realized Moby Doll wasn't interested in eating hands.
PHOTO BY DON MCLEOD, COURTESY OF TERRY MCLEOD.

The teeth that had terrified humans for years ... and the lesions that covered Moby's skin courtesy of the polluted water in the harbor. PHOTO BY DON MCLEOD, COURTESY OF TERRY MCLEOD.

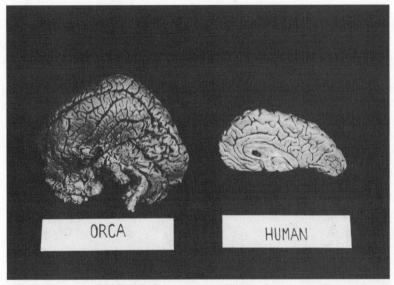

Scientist Paul Spong was fascinated by the complexity of Moby Doll's big brain and set it next to a relatively puny human brain to help convince Greenpeace to save the whales in 1975. PHOTO BY GREENPEACE CO-FOUNDER REX WEYLER.

Artist-harpoonist Sam Burich shows off an early version of the sculpture of his model and friend, Moby Doll. PHOTO BY JOE BAUER, COURTESY OF JUNE FLETCHER.

Friends and colleagues Murray Newman and Pat McGeer share their memories of Moby Doll at a symposium on Saturna Island in 2013, forty-nine years after their world-changing expedition. PHOTO BY CHARLES CAMPBELL.

CHAPTER ELEVEN

FEEDING TIME

"When that whale finally began eating the whole city
seemed to heave a great sigh of relief."
STUART KEATE, PUBLISHER OF THE *VANCOUVER SUN*

W ITH BURICH WORKING on the model, Newman trying to
find a new home for Moby, and McGeer juggling duties as
a scientist, a politician, and the world's first killer whale veterinarian, the aquarium needed the world's leading whale experts to
care for their million-dollar baby. So who else would they call but a
pair of fourteen-year-old boys?

Chris Angus would hop on his bike to meet his buddy Robin
Best, then the two would pedal along Vancouver's hilly west side
streets to reach the military base. Both boys had grown up loving
animals. Robin's dad, Alan Best, ran the zoo at Stanley Park. The
kids had volunteered to work at the children's zoo but eventually
decided to volunteer at the new aquarium next door because it featured something far more exotic than ducks—teenaged girls. After
the boys spotted the girls volunteering at the aquarium, their interests shifted to all things aquatic. When Moby Doll moved into their
neighborhood, the idea of whale watching for the aquarium was irre-
sistible—especially after they met Moby.

Chris had a ticket to see the Beatles make their Vancouver debut at Empire Stadium. This was cooler. He'd seen these whales in the wild before—and knew they were dangerous, knew what everyone did—that if he fell into the ocean with a killer, it was game over. But this was different; this was magic. He didn't see a monster. Chris saw something amazing. As he looked into the big round eye of the creature surfacing to stare at him, he recalled seeing lions at the circus. Lions were scary. He'd seen bulls on farms, and they were scary. When he'd seen those animals, his heart had started racing, the adrenaline was pumping, he was braced for anything. But here was the monster he'd grown up knowing could tear a lion to shreds, and as he and Robin looked at Moby and the whale looked back, the boys didn't sense any danger at all. The creature didn't seem to be eyeing them as food; it just seemed to be watching them the same way they were watching the whale. "We weren't scared," says Angus, "just fascinated."

It helped that by the time the boys met Moby, no one was still bracing for an attack. The boys watched as McGeer—a scientist they idolized—knelt on Burich's float, dipping the hydrophone into the water to record the whale. They saw Burich, Penfold, and Terry McLeod trying to feed the whale. If Moby wanted to eat a man, she certainly could.

The best part was that Newman worked his magic and convinced Chris and Robin they were a key part of the operation. They didn't just watch the whale; they were asked to take notes. What did she eat? Did her swimming pattern vary? Did she ever seem distressed? The responsibility was thrilling. "We really felt like budding scientists," says Angus.

The key player in the care and feeding of Moby now was McLeod. Like Newman, Bauer, and the boys, he had also been fascinated by all animals from an early age. Before joining the aquarium, McLeod had worked at the zoo for Robin's dad—also starting as a volunteer in his early teens. "I'd bring animals home to nurse them—the kinkajou, raccoons, baby squirrels, etcetera. I kept mom and dad busy," says

McLeod. In 1961, at age sixteen, McLeod started volunteering at the aquarium—first as a floor boy, which meant sweeping up after visitors, then working the 4 to 6 AM shift cleaning the reptile cages. By the time Moby was caught, the nineteen-year-old McLeod was officially billed as a "salt water aquarist" and "diver collector."

Then McLeod was asked to feed Moby. McLeod had never seen a killer whale before arriving at the Jericho pen. When he looked into the water, McLeod wasn't frightened either. He just saw another wounded animal that needed help. "After all the hoopla quieted down I took on the role as primary feeder and trainer," says McLeod. "I spent many hours in the daytime and then in the evening, coaxing and encouraging Moby to eat."

Although almost no one was allowed into the Jericho site, Moby's fame continued to spread. The *Toronto Star* reported that "the arrival of no other young female swimmer has ever so set a city on its ear since Marilyn Bell plowed across Lake Ontario to Toronto ten years ago. But this time the city was Vancouver, jewel of the Pacific, and the swimmer came from far out in the ocean—a 15-foot, three ton, lady killer whale." The National Film Board newsreel starring Moby was screened in more than forty countries.

As Moby became more famous, her history was rewritten to become more glamorous. A legend began taking shape, and the capture shifted from accidental to intentional to ingenious. The *Sun* revised Burich's role in Operation Killer Whale, telling readers, "it was Sam Burich who was on watch and he fired off a six-foot harpoon so skillfully it went through the back of Moby Doll's neck and she survived the attack." The missed kill shot had transformed into a spectacular feat of marksmanship.

Humorists offered their own take on the whale's tale. The *Province*'s Eric Nicol, one of Canada's most famous comic writers, imagined a conversation in which Moby's first words were, "Let's talk money... Fish work to scale, but I am a warm-blooded mammal."

Kathy Hassard, the *Sun*'s "women's news" writer, ran an "interview" translating the whale's chirps. Hassard's story stressed Moby's girlish charms and had the whale complaining, "No woman has been near me since I was harpooned... Strange men have talked to me and strange men have whistled at me, but I'm not that kind of girl."

WILLIAM SCHEVILL WASN'T just the foremost authority on whale sounds; he was a pioneer in sonar research. He was assisted by William Watkins, who Schevill described as a whale interpreter. The Harvard duo arrived for a two-day visit, determined to collect all the data they could. For the acoustics experts, Moby Doll was as priceless as Newman had boasted. This was a chance for researchers to do something that had seemed unimaginable only a few weeks earlier—study the calls of a killer whale.

Even before they heard Moby's squeaks, they had suspected that orcas and dolphins had a sophisticated form of communication. The military was particularly intrigued by their built-in sonar systems. The first time the Harvard men arrived to listen to Moby, she apparently wasn't interested in being recorded. The would-be Bo-Peep didn't peep. The researchers were disappointed but undeterred. Schevill told the *Province*, "Maybe it's because she's a girl. In whales, you know, the males are the gabby ones. The females are comparatively quiet."

He also wondered if perhaps captives were simply quieter than whales in the wild. Maybe Moby read the interview and decided to prove something, because after that first silent meeting she started chatting, and Schevill and Watkins kept their recorder rolling. Watkins told reporters he thought the clicking sounds were probably a form of echolocation and the other sounds were communication, possibly in response to the noises of nearby boats. But he wasn't sure what the whale was saying. "Trouble is we don't speak whale-ese."

When the *Sun* asked Schevill what Moby might be trying to communicate, he was less inclined to speculate on translations than cartoonists and columnists were—though he did suspect he'd learned one word in whale-ese. "We still can't interpret what the whale sounds mean, except for a few distinctive sounds which can mean something like 'ouch.'"

Schevill and Watkins arrived just as Newman was preparing his case to convince the aquarium's board of governors to fund a proper home for Moby. The Harvard stars made it for him. Schevill told reporters, "I hope you can find a proper place where everybody can see her... You have an exhibit here that nobody else has. And even if this whale should perish you have shown what can be done. The important thing for us is that we had never heard a killer whale before. Now we know what such a critter sounds like." They also told Newman and, more importantly, the media, that the critter looked healthy to them.

That night, Newman explained to the more fiscally cautious members of his board—in a message probably intended for the mayor and other critics—that the $20,000 offer from Marineland was contingent on the whale's health. Neither Marineland nor Undersea Gardens was prepared to gamble $20,000 on an exhibit that might be dying of starvation. This time, Newman didn't appeal to anyone's sense of scientific curiosity or philanthropy but argued that a healthy Moby Doll was worth a lot more in tourist dollars than $20,000. Bell-Irving backed him up. "From a financial point of view, if Moby Doll returns to good health, and barring any accident, we can't lose in investing in a permanent public showplace for her."

The board had no choice. Newman was authorized to find a permanent home for Moby, where she could swim in proper salt water in front of huge crowds of paying customers. A few days later, Burich unveiled a preliminary model of his sculpture—a playful five-foot version of the fifteen-foot whale. His whale appeared to be leaping to freedom.

AT THE END of August, Moby Doll was looking pale. She was losing her sheen—her slick black skin was turning gray. McGeer was concerned. The whale may have looked healthy to the acoustics researchers two weeks earlier, but this couldn't be a good sign. The experts from other marine parks told him to relax, that mammals changed color in fresher water.

Moby also had what appeared to be a fungal infection. Again, McGeer and Newman were worried that this had been caused by the water at Jericho. A skin specialist reassured them that the rash was nothing to worry about, and neither was Moby's paler skin tone. McGeer deferred to the experts and told reporters: "I hope all the people of British Columbia soon have a chance to see the killer whale." But McGeer and Newman still wanted the whale in saltier water ASAP—except they weren't just dealing with bureaucracy but with enough red tape to drown a humpback.

Even if Moby wasn't eating and her skin looked washed out, she hadn't looked healthier or happier since the day she had been captured. She had broken out of her repetitive swimming pattern and appeared to be playing. She started slapping her tail and splashing her visitors; then she started leaping. Moby must have been working up an appetite, because on September 8, guards were certain they saw her eat a fish from the line. The next day, Moby finally, definitively, ended her hunger strike.

Newman was meeting Ted Griffin from the Seattle Marine Aquarium and Allan Williams, chairman of the West Vancouver parks commission—and the prime candidate to host the whale's new pen. While Newman was chatting with Griffin, Williams tried holding the line for Moby, and for the first time, everyone could see her take the fish. Newman believed Williams was the first person to ever feed a killer whale. The small crowd at the pool cheered. Then Griffin fed the whale a cod. "It was electric," recalled Griffin half a century later in an interview with PBS. For Griffin, it was a sign that his childhood dream of having his own killer whale—perhaps even riding his own whale—hadn't been just a fantasy; he really did belong with these creatures. "From that point on, I knew I would risk everything, sacrifice everything, go to the end of the world to get a whale."

Newman and his delighted visitors watched as Moby quickly devoured another hundred pounds of cod and a salmon.

The *Sun* headline the next day was "Whale Eats." Newman was described as "elated." He was also relieved. For the first time since bringing Moby Doll to Vancouver, he could finally allow himself to believe she was going to be all right.

The next day, the aquarium staff tried feeding Moby from the float with a shorter line, and McGeer went back to stuffing salmon with extra vitamins to combat the fungal infection. CBC TV breathlessly reported: "Moby Doll has started eating in a big way. For the first time since her capture in July, the killer whale has started to take large quantities of food. Yesterday she ate about a hundred pounds of dead fish... Today she had a similar meal... The whale seems to be enjoying her meals. Each time a fish is offered she nuzzles it with her big snout before taking it from the line." Now that she was eating, Mobymania was back in full swing.

While Bell-Irving served a brief stint as Vancouver's acting mayor, he urged council to declare Moby Doll the city's new official symbol. He felt it would be appropriate, not just because of the whale's fame but because of her connection to the city's origins before the white settlers arrived—a radical concept in 1964. "It would also be distinctive because it is part of our native Indian mythology," he said.

Bell-Irving argued that any city could have a flower or bird represent it, but a coastal city should have an emblem that signified the coast—and killer whales were regularly seen in Vancouver's harbor. Aquarium boosterism aside, the whale certainly seemed like a more inspired choice than the outline of city hall, which was the image that currently graced the copper plates that were presented to distinguished guests. The proposal was prompted by the impending arrival of American president Lyndon Johnson. Bell-Irving hoped the president could meet the whale, and if that wasn't possible, that he could at least receive a miniature silver whale sculpture in honor of his visit.

Meanwhile, Moby's appetite remained front-page news. The *Sun* featured a photo of Moby eating and reported that she had consumed a forty-pound lingcod, a five-pound salmon, four five-pound red snappers, and (though this seems unlikely) a horse's heart and liver.

A few days later, Moby began approaching her keepers and waiting for them to drop fish into her mouth. She wasn't prepared to take food off a long string, but she'd eat if the men hand-fed her. When it was clear that Moby wouldn't try to eat her feeders along with her food, they stopped using lines and began hand-feeding the dreaded killer whale. The newspapers soon featured photos of Moby eating out of McLeod's hand, then Newman's.

Then Burich finally fed the whale. "Sam went from holding the food from the end of a pole to holding the food in his hand and having Moby come up and take it right out of his hand," said Newman. "When we realized we could feed it by hand and it wouldn't take our whole arm into its mouth, it was amazing."

Says McGeer, "When it started, everybody took a turn."

Newman began publicly musing about having Moby jump out of the water to take the fish, like the dolphins in Marineland. Moby was less enamored of that idea. When Penfold tried to get her to leap for her supper, she swam to the center of the pen in protest. Then Penfold offered a couple of orange rockfish. When Moby saw the fish, she swam to the center of the pool, swatted the water, and didn't come back to the float until Penfold offered another gray cod. After Penfold sliced the spines of the rock fish, Moby ate them. "By gosh," said Penfold. "She's training me." Moby also played with Penfold when he ventured underwater in his scuba gear—in the safety of a wire cage—to get a closer look at her skin infection. When he turned his back, Moby would nudge the cage, then dart away and squeal.

Bauer was one of the only regulars who didn't spend time trying to feed Moby. "I did pet it [the whale] one time, but I was always too busy taking pictures. One time I touched it when I was visiting Sam. Sam very definitely fell in love with it." Burich told reporters that the whale he'd called Hound Dog reminded him of "a great big cocker spaniel."

McLeod didn't feel like Moby was training him, but he knew she was bonding with him. After he started hand-feeding Moby, McLeod began rubbing her stomach—first with a broom, then with his hand. Soon he was scratching her fins and had Moby presenting a flipper and rolling over.

This was everything Newman had dreamed of and more. A killer whale liked getting belly rubs? The public would love that.

Everything was going so well that on September 29, the lead whale watchers finally took a break so that they could watch more whales—in the wild. Newman and McGeer went on a collecting expedition and brought Colonel Matthews to discuss how they might land another orca to keep Moby company—without the help of a lucky harpoon shot. After Newman and his crew observed several pods, they decided it would be a challenge to track whales without aerial support.

When his boat returned to shore, Newman was quizzed about rumors that he'd been trying to capture a new killer whale. Newman admitted he was intrigued by the idea of snagging a second whale— after he found Moby a proper home—but he wasn't sure how to go about it. "Catching a whale alive is more difficult than people would think. And how would we know if it is a male or female before we shot the harpoon?"

On October 3, the Mother of the Finback Whales died. While Newman and McGeer were whale watching, and Burich was sculpting another model, Maisie Hurley, who'd predicted Moby's imminent death and a disaster striking Vancouver, suffered a stroke. The extensive *Sun* coverage of her legacy politely ignored her prognostications about the fate of the whale, and no one suggested that perhaps the disaster she'd predicted was her own. Hurley was gone, and despite her dire warnings, Moby had never looked better—nor had the aquarium. As reports of Moby's ever-expanding menu filled the papers, the federal government committed $250,000 to an expansion, and the Vancouver Parks Board approved a $750,000 addition to the existing building. Newman had everything he needed—except a proper home for his whale.

On October 9, Moby Doll only took a pair of fish from McLeod at her 2 PM feeding. She had lost her appetite again and didn't seem to be swimming as smoothly as usual. Word went out to Moby's medical team that their favorite patient might be sick. As the aquarium's crew arrived to visit Moby, so did members of her pod.

Other orcas had visited before, but Bauer says that several whales clustered outside the pen, and this time it felt like something different was going on. "They were communicating, but Moby wasn't like her usual buoyant self." Then the pod swam away, and Bauer says Moby looked listless, tired, sad.

When McLeod tried feeding Moby again at three, he knelt on the platform to offer her a herring and she took the fish from his hand. But she only took one tiny fish. After a short swim around the pool, Moby came over to McLeod and waited for a back scratch, just like a puppy. McLeod gave her a brisk rub, and then Moby dropped quickly under the surface.

That was when bubbles began rolling up from below the water. This was unusual, but Moby was eating—perhaps it was nothing. It had to be nothing. A minute passed. Then two. Then three. Then hearts sank with their whale.

Bauer knew. "Either it was dead or escaped." And as Bauer looked at the still water, praying for Moby to surface inside or outside the pen, he knew that she hadn't escaped.

Moby exhaled through her blowhole for the last time, inhaled the brackish water, her lungs filled, and she suffocated—just as she would have the day she was harpooned if her family hadn't come to the rescue. After surviving a harpoon, gunfire, and a journey of nearly twenty hours tethered to the end of a rope, Moby Doll drowned.

The men watching Moby's pen couldn't believe what they were seeing. They kept hoping that, just maybe, their whale would leap out of the water to demand another treat, another belly scratch.

For months, everyone caring for Moby had braced for the worst, had expected it, but not after she started splashing them and playing with them and eating out of their hands. Not now. Not after they'd all fallen in love with her.

Newman was in a daze. He didn't want to talk to anyone, especially not the media. McGeer was devastated and angry. "It was like a death in the family."

McLeod, who'd fed Moby that last fish, felt "broken."

Bauer felt "shattered."

Burich stared at the dark water and the raft he'd spent so many days on, trying to convince Moby that she wasn't alone. He kept hoping she'd surface, or that just maybe she'd discovered a hole in her cage and escaped to freedom.

In 1964, men like Newman, McGeer, Burich, and Bauer didn't cry—at least not in public—but that didn't mean their hearts didn't break. Burich had lived up to his promise. Moby Doll—his victim, his model, his friend—was lying dead at his feet.

CHAPTER TWELVE

THE BLACKFISH GOLD RUSH

"Thank God Dr. Newman didn't want to do a model of a Roman circus, it would have been very hard on the Christians."

DAVID BEECHING, PROVINCIAL DIRECTOR, B.C. SPCA

JOE BAUER URGED the army divers to go into the murky water to get Moby. "The guys from the army were scared to go in," says Bauer. Even though they'd spent months with Moby, the military men were still wary of swimming with the ocean's most savage predator, just in case she was only playing dead. "They thought killer whale, killer whale, it's going to kill them. I told one guy, 'Look, it's an air-breather like we are. It's either escaped, or it's dead.'" No one believed the whale had escaped, but Bauer says it was two long hours before the military divers were brave enough to jump into the water. "Finally, the one guy figured I was right, so he went down and found it."

The diver put Moby Doll on one last leash, wrapping a strap around the whale's tail. At 5:15 PM, Moby surfaced for the final time, but it took a crane to lift the carcass.

The news leaked out that she was dead, but Newman didn't want anyone else coming through the gates into the pen. This couldn't be happening. Yes, Moby had lost her sheen, but she wasn't just eating, she was eating out of his hand. He had permission to find her a permanent home, a proper home. It wasn't fair. He'd just needed a bit more time.

CBC TV news, which had introduced the whale as a "dangerous monster," declared,

The most famous killer whale in the world, Vancouver's Moby Doll—is dead. The two-and-one-half ton mammal disappeared from the surface of the special pen shortly after she was fed at three o'clock this afternoon. The whale's body was hauled onto the dock at Jericho this evening, and it's being studied by a pathologist, a dermatologist, a bacteriologist, and Dr. Pat McGeer, who is a neuro-chemist. At this time it's believed that a lack of salt in the water was a major factor in the whale's death... It's reported that a diver has gone down in the waters of the Jericho pen to find out just what happened to the marine giant who endeared herself to thousands of people.

In a span of eighty-seven days, the dangerous monster had become Vancouver's beloved killer whale. And the people who'd set out to kill a whale were heartbroken.

Newman felt like he'd lost a prize specimen and a friend, and everyone wanted him to comment. He still had a whole aquarium full of exhibits, but nothing matched Moby. "Everything's falling apart. Moby Doll is dying and the whole world is moaning and people were wanting to know how I felt about it. 'How do you feel, Murray? Your whale's dead lying in the bottom of the pool, how do you feel?'" Newman had never been keen on talking about how he felt, but he was willing to share how it felt spending time with Moby, trying to understand the creature he considered the most magnificent on earth. "It really was impossible to believe how easy it was to be with," said Newman. "You could sit out there on Sam Burich's float and commune with the whale. It just became such a part of my life that losing it was a very serious emotional experience for me."

At a somber press conference at the Jericho officers' mess hall, Newman responded diplomatically to reporters and kept his feelings about what went wrong to himself. Then he went home to be with his family and his thoughts. Not long after Moby's death, Newman told reporters, "I loved that whale. I think that capturing it was the best thing that I ever did."

McGeer wasn't diplomatic. He lashed out at Vancouver's municipal government for not offering the support he believed could have saved the whale. "If proper facilities had been made available soon enough, Moby Doll would undoubtedly be alive today... Moby should have been moved long ago," he told reporters. "It's a real tragedy. Another case of 'for want of a nail, the shoe was lost.'" McGeer was furious and frustrated.

"We loved the creature and we were devastated when it died," he says. "It was a very sad experience because we thought this animal was going to live and it should have lived and we thought we'd have a proper home for it at the aquarium and it just didn't happen."

The *Province* ran the story on page one, underneath a banner headline saying, "Captive Mammal Calls it a Day." Obituaries ran in papers around the world, including the London *Times* and the *Sydney Morning Herald*. In a story titled "Lovable Killer Whale," *Life* magazine reported that "Once she [Moby] got over her shyness, she proved to be as playful and lovable as a puppy and almost as friendly."

One of Moby's medics, zoologist Dean Fisher, told *Reader's Digest* that Moby's story was the perfect antidote to other headlines of the day. "For a little while people found something better to worry about than the Cold War, the bomb and themselves. It was very refreshing."

The only break in the tension as Moby's body dangled above the water was when Burich decided to tease Bauer and asked if he still believed Moby was male. Bauer bristled. Even though almost no one else believed him, he knew what he'd seen in the water that first day off Saturna Island, and he'd never stopped grumbling about it to his friend as he read stories about what a proper "lady" Moby was. Bauer was adamant that he'd seen Moby's member in the waters off Saturna. "I got really quite close because I wanted to see where the harpoon went. So I could see something hanging and I thought it was guts and then I thought, 'How can that be gut? The harpoon went through the back.' So the next time the other whale moved a little bit more I saw what looked like a glans. I could see the head of the penis and everything else."

As Penfold stood next to the dead whale in his white lab coat, Burich said to Bauer, "Now's your chance to prove it." Bauer took the bait. He walked over to the whale, "and I put my hand in there and pulled it [the penis] out and said, 'Now what do you think, Vince?' and walked away." A reporter standing next to the scene had his headline. Most of the coverage of the whale's death featured variations on the news that Moby Doll should have been called Moby Dick, because no media outlet could resist the chance to make a dick joke.

AT THE NECROPSY, McGeer was assisted by Bigg, who was finding himself far more interested in orcas than he'd been in the seals and sea lions that were his official specialty. After finishing his PhD thesis on harbor seals and helping to relocate sea otters from Alaska to B.C., Bigg split his time between caring for these creatures and watching whales.

The examination confirmed what McGeer suspected. The harpoon wound had healed, but probably because the antibiotics were never delivered, the whale had a massive infestation of worms. Moby also had a skin condition, but as the dermatologists had assured McGeer, it wasn't fatal. The low salinity meant the harbor water wasn't buoyant enough, and Moby died of exhaustion, unable to remain afloat. The official cause of death was drowning. At death, the whale weighed 2,280 pounds and measured fifteen feet, four inches long. Once the gender was confirmed, the best guess was that Moby was two years old. Later estimates placed the orca's age as high as seven—which is still a child in the world of killer whales. It wasn't until 2011 that a study looking at the size and age of orcas made it easier to determine ages. John Ford says that based on that study, he believes Moby was probably five.

As he cut open the whale, McGeer made the same discovery that Bauer had and called to the others in the room, "Come over and see Moby Doll's dick."

McGeer admits that he first saw that part of Moby's anatomy a month earlier, when the dermatologist was examining the whale, and that he'd first heard about its existence weeks earlier. A four-year-old girl was watching Moby in the Jericho pen when she spotted something the silly grown-ups hadn't. The best part of "The Curator's New Clothes" story is that the scientist who publicly confirmed the whale's sex was the girl's dad, Vince Penfold. McGeer says Penfold told him the news not long after Moby moved to Jericho. "He called me in a panic about it. My response was to do nothing because it would eventually be found out by others." For the remainder of McGeer's political career, a prominent opposition politician regularly heckled him in the legislature by saying he wasn't to be trusted since he wasn't capable of sexing a whale.

The other secret that was finally revealed was why Newman and McGeer had been so confident when they announced the whale's sex. Even though Bauer (and later, McLeod) were sure they'd seen definitive proof the whale wasn't female, Marineland's general manager, William Monahan, examined the dorsal and assured Newman the whale was female. After Moby's death, Monahan admitted to reporters, "This isn't foolproof though, because both the male and female whales have the same shaped dorsals when they are young." Canadian whale expert Dr. Gordon Pike was equally convinced that the whale was female, and after Pike weighed in, even Bauer started second-guessing what he'd seen. "I was a young guy and Dr. Pike was one of my heroes." Bauer says he was told that another reason Penfold and others were certain Moby was female was that the whale had mammary glands—a reason he found baffling, since, as he notes, male humans have breasts too. But although some people knew Moby was male before the necropsy, even after the whale's death, "experts" still weren't always 100 percent sure how to determine a whale's sex shy of cutting the creature open.

After the dissection, parts of the whale were parceled off to doctors and researchers, as promised. Bigg, who'd assisted with the necropsy, was assigned to prepare the skeleton for exhibit. Once every bone and organ was claimed, the rest of Moby's remains became pet food. "It was properly disposed of," says Bauer. "It wasn't thrown away like garbage; it was all used."

In an interview with CBC TV, Newman vowed the aquarium would learn at least as much from studying Moby's corpse as it had from watching the live whale. It seemed like a hollow boast, a last bit of bravado for the cameras. But Newman had an aquarium to run, and animal lovers around the world—and especially the people of Vancouver—were mourning Moby Doll. Even if Newman didn't believe what he was telling the reporters, it was what he had to say.

BURICH HAD A sculpture to finish that would now be a memorial to the first killer whale ever displayed in captivity. It was clear Moby Doll would not be the last. Based on both Moby's behavior and the public's response, exhibitors around the world wanted their own killer whales.

Newman was certain he'd learned enough from the life and death of Moby Doll to care for any future captives. "These animals are fascinating," Newman told CBC TV. "The killer whale—Orcinus orca—is found in great abundance along the coast of British Columbia. It's the only place in the world where a human population lives in conjunction with a population of killer whales, and the entire world has focused attention on us for capturing this animal. And I would very much like to capture several of these animals. If I could keep them under good conditions, I'm sure that they would live and be healthy and active, and I think that it would be possible to exhibit them to the public."

Newman made a point of boasting to the media that despite assumptions to the contrary, Moby hadn't cost taxpayers a cent—at least not directly. The whale's housing and transportation had been covered by donations of materials, space, and labor. Alderman Bell-Irving told city council the aquarium was devising plans to create a proper home for its next whale. Bell-Irving also offered an apology of sorts for McGeer's attacks on council, blaming the delays in finding a safe space for Moby on the aquarium board he helped run. Bell-Irving, who'd been one of the most passionate advocates for finding a home for the whale, wasn't just trying to smooth things over ' with his fellow councilors but was also firing a shot across the bow of aquarium board members who'd been lukewarm in their support for funding a proper facility for Moby Doll.

The SPCA issued a statement declaring that the public should condemn any further attempts to capture and display a killer whale, mainly, it seemed, because the aquarium was unable to keep one alive. D. Blair of Victoria wrote the *Sun* to condemn the "crucifixion" of the killer. "No doubt some fault will be found in the machinery of Moby Doll's body which will account for this creature's death, account, that is, to the satisfaction of 'the highest and most intelligent of creatures.' But some may ponder, dull-witted and insensitive as we are, whether Moby Doll's crucifixion at the hands of the pygmies (if the pygmies will pardon the aspersion) has not just gone beyond the point of mortal tolerance."

Newman told the media he hoped to catch another killer whale as soon as he could build a space capable of housing one. "No Aquarium specimen ever emotionally affected people as much as did our captive killer whale, Moby Doll." But he wasn't convinced other killer whales would be as tame as Moby. "I worry about this sentimentalizing," he told reporters. "It was a nice whale, but it was still a predatory, carnivorous creature. It could swallow you alive." Newman also reminded the media that eighteen thousand whales had been killed worldwide that year. The implication was that the loss of a single whale shouldn't be viewed as such a tragedy. But this wasn't just any whale; this was Moby Doll—the world's whale. Newman later refined his public response, but he still believed his whale was unique. "The next one may not be the same," he warned the reporter for *Life* magazine. "Moby Doll was extraordinarily tame. Most of them would probably eat us if they got the chance. Gently, of course."

NEWMAN MAY NOT have been as obsessed as Ahab before meeting Moby, but he was now. The Vancouver Visitors Bureau declared Newman "Man of the Year" for not only landing a whale but also hooking national and international headlines in the world's most popular and prestigious media outlets. Moby was featured in *Time, Newsweek, Life,* the *Christian Science Monitor, Reader's Digest,* the London *Times,* the *New York Times,* and smaller newspapers everywhere. The whale's story was told on Canadian television, international radio broadcasts, and via the National Film Board's newsreel.

Newman wanted another killer whale for Vancouver. He wanted a chance to prove that he and his team had learned enough to care for a killer whale, that they'd learned enough to train one. But Newman wasn't the only person obsessed with catching a killer.

Marineland's captains weren't thrilled at being shown up by the bumbling Canadians. Victoria's Charlie White still wanted a killer whale as the centerpiece of his Undersea Gardens. Seattle's Ted Griffin had attempted captures in the past and certainly wasn't going to stop now. Other aquarists around the world were equally inspired, or embarrassed, that an amateur crew in Canada had accidentally done something they'd not only believed but publicly stated was impossible.

Maybe no one else agreed with Newman's assessment that Moby was worth $1 million, but $20,000 was certainly a big enough prize to get the attention of a lot of fishermen. Considering how much money exhibitors eventually made displaying killer whales, Newman's estimate was on the low side.

Less than a year after Moby's death, salmon fisherman Bill Lechkobit was caught in a storm near the small fishing village of Namu, B.C., and had to cut loose his net. The next day, he and his friend Bob McGarvey went to retrieve their gear and found a pair of killer whales tangled in their trap—an adult (twenty-two feet long) and a juvenile (ten feet long). A year earlier, they might have shot the monsters. Now they wanted to sell their catch for those big bucks they'd been reading about in the big-city papers—$25,000 a whale.

The Department of Fisheries offered Newman a flight to Namu so that he could meet the fishermen. Newman was hoping he could charm them into a more reasonable price. "When we arrived in Namu, I strolled out to the dock to talk to the young fishermen who possessed the whale and took a bottle of whisky out of my bag so we could share a congenial drink. When they declined and exclaimed that they did not drink, I knew I was in trouble." The fact that he was only offering $1,000 a whale might not have helped put the fishermen in a drinking mood.

Back in Vancouver, Newman was set to attend a black-tie banquet honoring his patron H.R. MacMillan. He buttoned his tux to prepare for battle and trolled the ballroom trying to find sponsors willing to help him land the whales. He tried appealing to hometown pride—warning that it would be humiliating for B.C. whales to end up in the U.S.—but he couldn't find anyone proud enough of their hometown to cut him a whale-worthy check.

The fishermen shared the stories of a bidding war with the newspapers. They claimed Marineland made an offer, "but it wasn't a very good one." They said other bidders in the pool included Griffin, White, and the New York World's Fair. While the fishermen played hard to get, their smaller whale—the one every aquarium wanted—slipped out of their net. Most of the bidders backed out, and suddenly the remaining whale was available at a deep discount. The fishermen weren't just afraid that the bigger whale might escape; they couldn't afford to take more time off work. The men wanted to sell their captive quickly—and they wanted cash. They'd settle for $8,000, and if they didn't receive it within twenty-four hours, the fishermen would cut the whale loose. It was a Saturday, and in 1965 banks weren't open on weekends.

While Newman tried to find a big fish to buy a whale, Griffin visited the businessmen and the bars on Seattle's waterfront where his aquarium was based and asked everyone to cough up some cash. He convinced his neighbors on the pier that if his aquarium had a whale, all of them would get rich. It was crowdfunding at its finest.

Soon Griffin filled a sack with $8,000 in crumpled bills. He chartered a floatplane to Namu and hired a former Canadian Mountie to serve as his bodyguard. Griffin said the fishermen were surprised by his arrival and challenged him to arm-wrestle before they agreed to the sale. After ransoming the whale, Griffin approached Don Goldsberry of the Tacoma Aquarium to help transport his catch to Seattle in a floating cage—much like the way the dry dock had transported Moby Doll. Unlike Newman, he didn't wait to name his prize. Griffin told the media his whale's name was Namu, in honor of the place it was caught.

Like Barnum, Griffin turned his whale's journey into a publicity tour and drummed up press at every stop on the nineteen-day, four-hundred-mile journey. Members of the media weren't the only ones watching. The whale's family members—believed to be an older female and a pair of calves—swam beside the cage. That led to Griffin's most ingenious PR coup. When another whale appeared and kept getting between the cage and its companions, Griffin said the new whale was stealing Namu's family and dubbed it "Oil Can Harry." Pure Barnum.

When Namu arrived in Seattle's harbor on July 28, he was greeted by a Dixieland band and go-go dancers. There were thousands of onlookers—and two protesters carrying signs pleading for the whale to be set free. It was as if Griffin had shown up with King Kong. That first day, his aquarium hosted five thousand paying customers to meet the new, twenty-five-foot-long, 7,520-pound star. Within two months, Griffin was living his dream of riding a whale. He told people the whole point of charging admission was so that he could afford his own pet killer whale.

Newman was publicly gracious—he lent Griffin his new biologist, Gil Hewlett—and privately jealous as he watched Namumania explode. Namu launched a song, a dance, and a Hollywood movie.

Griffin received $50,000 for the movie rights. Written by Arthur Weiss, creator of *Flipper* (the hit 1960s TV series about a lovable and heroic dolphin) and later the mastermind behind the cartoon *Super Friends*, *Namu, The Killer Whale* combined elements of Namu's story with Moby's and was built around the idea that whales weren't monsters; they were just misunderstood.

The Disneyesque movie begins with rapacious fishermen shooting at fierce killer whales. In an opening confrontation straight out of a spaghetti Western, there's a showdown in the town store, where the head fisherman, Clausen, confronts the scientist who wants to study the killer. "Look, you," says the fisherman, "we got nothin' against you science fellas comin' up here doing your work. I got nothing against rockets going up there to the moon. Down here in the sea that's hard facts. We make a living off of it. You don't know what kind of killer fish you're dealing with."

His sidekick agrees. "Mister, there ain't no fish in the world like that one. Blowing and a jumping right out of the water at you. He's pure killer!"

The third fisherman, playing a classic Gabby Hayes Western sidekick, chimes in. "That's right, mister. I've seen the big ones, all of 'em—sperm, finback, bowhead, and plenty of killer. Heard tell of a man fell over the side once, killers down below. Only half a man came up. They're bad, mister, real bad."

After being regaled by horror stories about the monster he's unleashed on the town, the square-jawed hero finally replies, "Did you ever see a man who'd been chewed up by a killer whale? I mean, actually, did you ever see one? Heard tell this, heard tell that. You heard tell. Right, Burt? It's a lot of nonsense. Nobody knows anything about killer whales. They've never had a chance to study them. I think it's about time they did."

Murray and Kathy Newman, Pat and Edith McGeer, and Vince Penfold went on a road trip to Seattle to meet the whale they believed should have been theirs. Newman also watched as Griffin and his partner, Goldsberry, set out to catch a companion for Namu.

Namu was the whale that launched a thousand ships—looking to catch more killer whales.

Griffin and Goldsberry initially tried to capture a whale just like Newman had—with a harpoon gun—but theirs was portable. They hopped a helicopter, spotted a female traveling with a baby, and took a shot. Their harpoon did exactly what Sam Burich's was supposed to—it killed the whale. They towed the dead whale into the secluded area of Rich Cove, Washington, with the orphaned calf following behind. The hunters decided to keep the baby but conceal the way they'd caught it. Goldsberry and Griffin—the man who had dreamed of swimming with killer whales—wrapped an anchor around the mother's corpse and sank it. It was the beginning of an age Hewlett and author Daniel Francis would dub "the era of the orca cowboys."

After the baby was placed in the pen, the young whale bit and bumped Namu. When Griffin got into the pool, the baby rammed him too. Griffin thought the new whale was going to hurt his prize exhibit and contacted the managers at SeaWorld, who'd wanted to buy Namu. He offered to lease them the fourteen-foot baby for $2,000 a month for the duration of the whale's life. SeaWorld wanted the whale, but they also wanted the name. The whale was for sale, but the legend of Namu wasn't. To capitalize on the brand Griffin was building, SeaWorld named their new star Shamu—the "she" version of Namu—and flew their killer to San Diego. It was the start of the blackfish gold rush.

On July 9, 1966, eleven months after arriving in Seattle, Namu became disoriented and tangled himself in the steel net of the pen. A necropsy determined he'd been poisoned by the polluted water. Griffin was devastated. From the moment he'd bought Namu, he'd rarely left the whale's side. As the whale's body was examined, Namu surprised the scientists just as Moby's had. This time, they'd guessed the correct sex, but when they dissected Namu, Griffin's team discovered a bullet from a Springfield rifle that appeared to have been lodged there for about ten years. Twenty-five percent of all killer whales captured for aquariums in the 1960s and 1970s had bullet wounds. After being dissected, Seattle's supersized superstar was chopped up into chicken feed.

Griffin and Goldsberry soon accomplished what the Franks had failed at—finding a way to capture killer whales. Griffin said later, "I continued to capture whales, but my heart was never in it again." When Griffin and Goldsberry became serious whale wranglers, one of their first customers was the U.S. Navy, which bought a pair in the hope that they could be trained for military duties such as recovering torpedoes. Newman had also been corresponding with the U.S. Navy and knew about its interest in enlisting orcas.

Shamu the First survived for six years, setting a new record for whales in captivity. But SeaWorld had learned from Marineland's experience with Bubbles the pilot whale, and Griffin and Newman's PR nightmares with Namu and Moby. Shamu never dies. As with James Bond, there is always another actor prepared to step—or swim—into the iconic role.

After Namu begat Shamu, Griffin and Goldsberry caught the next world-changing whale—Walter. On February 15, 1967, the cowboys corralled fifteen killer whales in Yukon Harbor, Washington. Two whales drowned, and the hunters released five because they were deemed too large to display. Two were going to SeaWorld and two were staying with Griffin, but one was available for sale. Newman went to meet the whales but didn't bite. It was tempting, but he didn't have the money to buy a killer whale or a place to put it. Of course, Newman wanted a whale, but he had built his tank for dolphins, not orcas. He wanted a killer whale, but he wanted to construct a proper space to display one first.

Then Griffin baited the hook by displaying Walter at the Vancouver Boat Trailer and Sports Show. There was a captive whale in Vancouver, and Griffin was offering it to Newman. McGeer, who was now on the aquarium's board, wanted a whale too. Bob McLaren, who'd been with Newman on the flight to Saturna to meet Moby, was now chairman. The aquarium was buying a whale.

Newman and Griffin agreed on a price of $22,000—on an install-ment plan. The payments would stop if Walter died. More than 100,000 people saw the whale in a tiny tank at the boat show. In 1967, three years after Moby was a memory, the aquarium purchased Wal-ter from Ted Griffin, the undisputed expert on captive whales. This time, the SPCA didn't hesitate to condemn the whole idea of captivity.

Instead of inoculating their new whale with a ten-foot pole, New-man's scientists examined their specimen up close, which led to the discovery that Walter needed a new name to go with her newly dis-covered sex. After a radio contest drew nearly six thousand entries, the judges settled on a suggestion from a six-year-old girl, who offered the name of her father's boat. It was the Haida word for killer whale—skana.

The same year Skana arrived in Vancouver, B.C.'s whaling sta-tion at Coal Harbour closed because, as predicted, there were now too few whales remaining on the West Coast for whaling to remain profitable.

When the aquarium's expansion was unveiled in 1967, Moby Doll finally took up residence on the ceiling of the newly opened British Columbia Hall. But the Moby model wasn't nearly as interesting to visitors as the live whale swimming in the tank outside.

IN 1970, GRIFFIN and Goldsberry went whale hunting in Penn Cove, just north of Seattle, Washington. For whale lovers, Penn Cove is Orca Altamont. Goldsberry herded eighty whales into a net. A super-pod. When protesters slit the nets to try to free the whales, at least three young whales were tangled in the net and drowned. In the past, dead whales were reported to authorities and sold to rendering plants—at least they were supposed to be reported to authorities. But now that the stakes were higher, people loved whales, and aquar-iums loved buying them for top dollar, the hunters didn't want word to get out. So Goldsberry's divers slit the corpses open and weighed the dead whales down with chains.

Jason Colby, a history professor at the University of Victoria who's writing a book about the cultural evolution of our relationship with orcas, says the tragic incident was rife with irony. "Griffin released nearly all of the whales and didn't intentionally kill any of them. And even if he had killed them all, he would not have broken the law—strange though that might seem to us now. It is also worth noting that he let the others go, despite several outstanding orders from customers. From this perspective, it is strange to think that the real tragedy of Penn Cove may be that none of the eighty would have likely died if the activists had not intervened. The road to ruin and all that, eh?"

Griffin was meeting with Washington governor Dan Evans to discuss a proposal that would ban the capture of live whales in Washington waters, when the three dead baby orcas washed up onshore. "I remember sitting with Dan and his administrative assistant came in and informed him that the news story had just broken. And Dan asked me the circumstances, and I explained and said that I would not pursue the issue at that time. And the legislation was passed, and that was the beginning of the ending of the live capture of killer whales in Puget Sound." It was also the end of Griffin's career as a whale hunter. Killing whales might have been bad PR, but covering up the deaths was whale Watergate.

Meanwhile, the world was becoming more attuned to whales. In 1970, American scientist Roger Payne released his recordings of Bermuda's humpbacks as the album *Songs of the Humpback Whale*. In 1971, the album cracked America's *Billboard* charts and stayed there for eight weeks.

By 1973, forty-eight killer whales, mostly babies and juveniles, had been captured in the waters off Washington and B.C., and at least a dozen were known to have died as a result of attempted captures. The southern residents had lost a generation. That year the price for a captive killer reached $70,000—which would translate into about $400,000 in 2016.

In 1975, Bob Wright from Victoria's Sealand captured a half dozen killers at Pedder Bay on southern Vancouver Island and, after taking one for himself, was planning to sell the others. A fourteen-foot male was flown to New York. That's when Greenpeace threatened to organize a boycott of Air Canada, which was set to carry the other orcas to their new homes and threatened to distribute bumper stickers that read: "Air Canada Kills Whales!" As tempers flared, police arrested a protester who tried to cut the net holding the captives. The remaining whales were released because, under Canadian law, they were too small to be sold. A month later, the B.C. government declared a moratorium on all future captures of killer whales in the province's waters.

In March 1976, Goldsberry's hunting party was caught herding killer whales into Washington's Budd Inlet using helicopters, speedboats, and explosives. If Goldsberry was looking for trouble, his timing was impeccable. Ralph Munro, assistant to Washington governor Dan Evans, was fishing in the area with his wife and two other couples when the hunters chased a half dozen whales into their net. Meanwhile, Washington's Evergreen State College was hosting the world's first Orca Symposium.

Evans sued SeaWorld, and the courts ordered Goldsberry to free "the Budd Inlet Six." The incident inspired Washington State senator Warren Magnuson to push the American federal government to outlaw killer whale captures in U.S. waters. The law never passed, but the rodeo was over for the orca cowboys—at least in North America. SeaWorld and Goldsberry moved their whale-rustling routine to Iceland.

That same year, just two summers after *Jaws* scared almost everyone out of the ocean, Hollywood tried to ride the scary sea monster wave and released *Orca: The Killer Whale*, which updated Melville's *Moby-Dick*. The killer even bit off someone's leg—Bo Derek's, a few years before she became a global sex symbol as the original "perfect ten."

Whether the movie sank at the box office because it was impossible to believe in evil whales in the age of Shamu, or because even the shark from *Jaws* would have had a tough time swallowing a plot where a whale tried to topple a ship with an iceberg—it was clear that the image of the dangerous killer whale had vanished, replaced by the idea of a smart, sympathetic mammal. The great white shark in *Jaws* was a relentless killing machine. The whale in *Orca* was equally savage but had a motive that went beyond blood lust—he was avenging the death of his pregnant mate.

Even Hollywood didn't try to paint killer whales as villains. Instead of a monster movie, *Orca* could have been a Greenpeace recruitment tool, since it featured whalers slaughtering mates and babies as bait to catch bigger whales.

CHAPTER THIRTEEN

THE FIRST ORCA

"I wonder what that thing is thinking with my brain."
DR. PAT MCGEER

P AT MCGEER HAD fallen in love with Moby Doll. He'd been thrilled when he was able to feed the legendary predator by hand. But this was the moment he'd signed on for. Even though he'd never operated on anything this size before, McGeer knew how to slice open the whale's skull and remove his prize.

He extracted Moby's brain himself, by hand, using a bone saw. The orca's big brain was bigger than he had hoped—five times the size of a human's and weighing in at nearly fifteen pounds. And this was from a young whale, not a mature adult. The brain was also more complicated than McGeer had imagined—more complicated than a human brain. Dolphin brains were impressive, but this brain was spectacular.

McGeer followed the same protocols he used for his human specimens. "We treated it by the standard procedures. It was weighed and placed on crushed ice." A lot of crushed ice. "We were particularly interested in doing biochemistry on the hypothalamus and pituitary to determine if the brain, and what parts of it, could synthesize adrenalin," says McGeer. He didn't use any special tools to work with the whale, because there were no special tools to use.

The serious scientific surprise was the size of the auditory nerve, which was considerably larger than the optic nerve, revealing to a delighted McGeer that unlike humans, whales relied more on sound than sight. This brain also operated on more levels than a human's. The whale required the additional complexity to manage additional senses. Humans don't have sonar. And there were far more cortical folds—the lines in a brain that were considered a key indicator of intelligence, at least back when scientists thought humans had the brain with the most intricate cortical folds.

It wasn't easy to move more than two thousand pounds of dead mammal, so the dissection was performed at the military base. During the examination, McGeer discovered that Moby may have suffered some brain damage when he was harpooned. The concussion that almost caused him to drown was the result of a minor skull fracture. In a paper McGeer and Newman coauthored for *Zoologica* (the official publication of the New York Zoological Society), they revealed how miraculous the accidental capture had been. "It was extremely lucky that this particular animal was not killed by the initial harpoon shot. Had the harpoon struck slightly caudally, it would have penetrated the cervical cord. Slightly rostrally, it would have penetrated the brain."

They also believed they now knew why their whale had been so docile. Their conclusion: "The immaturity, wounded condition and isolation of the animal probably affected its behaviour considerably. Its immaturity may have accounted for its lack of aggressiveness." Moby may not have been dangerous, but that didn't mean other killer whales wouldn't attack humans if given the chance. Based on their knowledge of how these monsters attacked other mammals, they still believed Moby was an anomaly.

BY THE TIME Skana arrived at the Vancouver Aquarium, no one was still expecting killer whales to eat their trainers. Now that he finally had a live killer whale on display, Newman was determined to do anything he could to keep her healthy and happy—and to learn as much as possible from his new specimen. Newman wanted to train Skana to do tricks, but he also wanted to prove that his aquarium wasn't SeaWorld or Marineland. Yes, his whale would put on a show, but Skana wouldn't just be an entertainer; she'd be an educator.

Terry McLeod, who'd fed and cared for Moby, became Skana's head trainer. But in choosing a leader for the research team, McGeer wanted to try something completely different. According to Newman, "Pat had the idea that we should have a new approach and really go in a different direction in science, not just natural history. I was interested in natural history and ecology and environmental physiology and stuff like this. And Pat said, 'We should be more modern, we should be involved with psychology and understanding animal intelligence.'" Yes, Newman was still trying to sell thousands of tickets a day to families wanting to watch his whale, but he wasn't dressing Skana up like Santa Claus or Uncle Sam—he wanted to do actual research. McGeer had an off-the-wall idea for studying the animal—instead of a zoologist, why not hire someone familiar with human behavior?

Paul Spong was a twenty-eight-year-old New Zealander who'd gone California flower child while studying human brains for his postdoctoral work at UCLA. Says Spong, "I had a friend in the Psychology Department at UBC who told me there were no jobs vacant there but one that was in the Psychiatry Department, involving half-time neurophysiological research in a lab on the campus and half-time behavioural research with a newly captured orca at the aquarium."

Newman recalled that, "Paul came along and he liked the aquarium a lot more than he liked the university, so he was at the aquarium all the time." Since there were already experts studying orca acoustics—the Harvard scientists had released a paper based on their time with Moby—Newman and McGeer asked Spong to study the whale's vision.

Although Spong had lived in New Zealand and California, where the waters contained plenty of killer whales, he had never seen one before meeting Skana, knew nothing about them, and had no

particular interest in animals. Spong says, "I never imagined working with animals before I applied for a job at the aquarium." Spong
assumed he would be working with a huge aquatic lab rat. But from
the moment Spong arrived, he was intrigued by the idea of working
with a whale.

It wasn't Skana who initially caught Spong's attention, though. It
was Moby Doll.

"I walked into Dr. Pat McGeer's lab on the UBC campus, and the
first thing that I encountered was this huge jar with a massive brain
sitting in the corner. That was the brain of Moby Doll. It was, to me, a
startling moment because on the shelf above this jar were a bunch of
smaller jars with human brains in them. My first thought was what
does this animal do with this brain?" As Spong studied the huge
brain, it was apparent that the gray matter was far more complex
than our own.

The more Spong tested Skana's reactions to visual cues, the
more convinced he became that the whale was testing him. Spong
was asking Skana to identify images from two cards and reward-
ing the whale with food for the correct answer. After figuring out
the answers Spong was looking for and giving the correct ones for
weeks, Skana gave Spong the wrong answer—eighty-three times in a
row. Skana wasn't just playing with Spong—she was joking with him.
Instead of seeing a lab rat, Spong began to see an equal—with a sense
of humor. "I started to think, I'd better get to know who this whale is."

Even though he was still wary of Skana, Spong began dangling his
feet in the water to touch the whale. "On one morning, Skana came
over to me as she normally did and touched my bare feet and suddenly opened her jaws and slashed them across my feet, so I could
feel her teeth across the tops and bottoms of my feet. Naturally, I
jerked my feet out of the water. Eventually, I put my feet back in the
water." When he dipped his feet back in, Skana repeated her behavior. So did Spong. After nearly a dozen repetitions of the same scene,
Spong stopped flinching and Skana stopped grazing him. Spong realized he was no longer afraid of the whale and that the whale wasn't

warning him; she was training him and, just maybe, reminding him who was really in charge.

In 1968, the Vancouver Aquarium finally caught a whale on purpose. The young male, named Hyak, was initially kept in a separate pool from Skana. Spong thought Hyak seemed depressed. After working with traditional rewards of fish, Spong began experimenting. Instead of presenting Skana and Hyak with food for a correct answer, he'd offer music, trying to share human culture with the whales. To get Hyak to vocalize, Spong rewarded the whale with three minutes of music, ranging from Mozart to the Moody Blues. Spong soon became convinced the music was working as a reward, convinced the whale was listening. Perhaps the most fascinating discovery was that both Hyak and Skana responded best when the songs changed—which indicated the whales had a phenomenal acoustic memory. Hyak quickly demonstrated a taste for modern music and performed an energetic exhibition when he first heard the Rolling Stones. Hyak was especially intrigued by live music and would cozy up next to acoustic guitars that were played for him. These were not the reactions of lab rats. Spong began questioning the ethics of keeping anything that jumped so joyfully to "Jumpin' Jack Flash" in captivity—and he started saying so publicly.

The more Spong worked with Skana and Hyak, the more convinced he was that these creatures were as intelligent as humans—but that his subjects had a different kind of intelligence. He began refusing to call Skana and Hyak killer whales and would only refer to them as orcas. "At a certain point, I felt I understood enough about the nature of this creature that it felt unfair to call it 'killer,'" says Spong. "I felt at the time that if it was appropriate to call this whale 'killer whale,' then perhaps we should call ourselves 'killer apes.'" It's a point Spong has never stopped being passionate about. Although most scientists still prefer the term "killer whale," anyone working with Spong knows they had better stick to "orca."

In June 1969, when Spong's contract came up for renewal, Newman let it lapse. Spong was no longer just thinking outside the box, he was thinking outside the tank. The killer whales were the biggest draws at the aquarium, and Spong wanted to set them free. After he finished working inside the aquarium Spong took up residence outside—demanding Skana's release. With his long hair and picket sign, Spong looked more at home protesting outside the building than working inside the lab.

In 1970, Spong moved to Hanson Island, an isolated community near northern Vancouver Island, to run his own research facility, OrcaLab, and track the lives of the northern residents and transients.

As his fascination with whales grew, Spong wanted to find some-one who would help him protect Skana's family, so he approached an activist group that had been founded in Vancouver in 1971 to protest nuclear testing—Greenpeace. A collection of journalists, Quakers, and hippies, originally known as the Don't Make a Wave Commit-tee, set out to stop a U.S. nuclear weapons test near Alaska by sailing their boat, the *Greenpeace*, to the test site. Their first mission was a failure—the U.S. Navy intercepted them en route to Alaska—but the concept was a hit. Joni Mitchell, James Taylor, Chilliwack, and Phil Ochs helped fund their first voyage with a benefit concert, and the idea of a group campaigning to save the environment caught on quickly in Vancouver, which was a hotbed of the Canadian counter-culture movement and a popular destination for Americans dodging the Vietnam draft. One of the first people to sign up with Green-peace was McGeer. "I wanted the pollution in the water around Vancouver harbor cleaned up because the water we swam in was dirty, and nobody was doing anything about it, and I thought maybe Greenpeace would do something. So I was one of the first people to join." He was also one of the first people to quit. "I thought they were a little bit extreme."

Greenpeace was known for its direct action techniques, which Spong hoped the group might use to combat whaling. Spong knew exactly how to convince Greenpeace to save the whales. He'd intro-duce the leaders to Skana. One of Greenpeace's earliest members, Paul Watson, says they'd sneak into the aquarium after it was closed to swim with Skana. Watson had been warned about killers when he was in the coast guard in the late sixties. "I had a coast guard captain telling me that those orcas, he'd seen them eat people," says Watson. "Of course, there's no authenticated case of an orca attacking a person, but this guy was absolutely convinced that they ate people."

Spong doesn't recall swimming with Skana, but he was determined to take Greenpeace co-founder Bob Hunter to meet the whale. The catch? Spong needed to get back inside the institution he'd picketed—and he needed an invitation. A reporter from *Time* magazine contacted Newman and asked to photograph the scientist with Skana. Spong wanted to convince Greenpeace to save the whales, and to do that he had to visit the whale who had changed his life. The plan was to announce the campaign to save the whales in front of the pool holding the whale he'd fought to free.

Newman considered the request to host the city's first truly influential anti-captivity protester, the scientist who'd publicly attacked the institution he'd given his life to and...agreed. His only condition was that Spong promise that the event would stick to the issue of saving the whales in the wild, not releasing Skana.

On October 18, 1974, Spong stood by the edge of his old friend's pool and played his flute for Skana—and the *Time* photographer. Then Skana spy-hopped right beside Hunter and checked out the Greenpeace guru. Spong told Hunter to stick his head in Skana's mouth. But Hunter had no interest in testing Spong's faith in this creature and declined. Spong urged him again. Finally, somehow, Spong convinced Hunter to put his head into Skana's open mouth. What happened next was one of those moments that convince researchers that orcas operate on levels we may never understand.

The killer whale closed her mouth around Hunter's head—just enough for the Greenpeace co-founder to know, without a doubt, that his life was at her mercy. A few moments later, Skana opened her jaws to release him, and when Hunter removed his head, his mind was officially blown. His life, like Spong's, now belonged to the whales.

Hunter cited the experience as the pivotal moment when he found the cause that redefined his life and soon reinvented

Greenpeace. "Hunter was now ready to mount an anti-whaling crusade," Greenpeace co-founder Rex Weyler recalled in his book about the early days of the organization. "Initially, he was unable to persuade Greenpeace to embrace the cause. Nevertheless, he and Spong were both obsessed with the idea. They developed a strategy they thought might stop the whalers while also delivering images of the horrors of whaling into living rooms around the world. They would harass whaling ships in small inflatable motor boats and film the confrontations. Within a few months, Spong and Hunter's enthusiasm had become infectious, and the other members of Greenpeace agreed to mount a protest in 1975. And they have been doing it ever since."

Weyler says Spong became

the unofficial leader of the green faction of Greenpeace. Within Greenpeace at the time there existed a slight rift between the faction that believed Greenpeace should stay focused on the nuclear issues, stopping nuclear bomb tests, and those who wanted to do more explicit ecology actions. We used to say, "We need to put the Green in Greenpeace." Ironically, today, I've heard people say, "We need to put the Peace back into Greenpeace." In any case, there was this split, and the ecology group actually formed a separate group, the Stop Ahab Committee, which functioned quasi-independently for a while, but as this faction gained success with the public, it eventually became the driving force of Greenpeace.

Challenging nuclear testing was abstract—and not all that popular with American political leaders—but humans risking their lives to stop Russian whalers at the height of the Cold War, and placing their small boats next to huge whale carcasses—that was unambiguously heroic, the stuff of legends.

Weyler says Spong demonstrated the intelligence of whales by showing off a whale's big brain. Spong "borrowed" Moby Doll's brain from McGeer's lab and took it to Weyler's house to photograph.

The Greenpeace founders took photos of Moby's brain next to a human's to show how big it was and to make their case that whales deserved to be protected. The photos of the two brains accompanied a newspaper story on Greenpeace that was published in Vancouver just before their first big anti-whaling event.

IN 1982, GREENPEACE helped win an international moratorium on commercial whaling that finally went into full effect in 1986.

Spong continues to be a passionate and vocal advocate for the rights of Skana's people and a leader in the fight to free captive whales—especially Corky (the second), a member of A5 pod (a northern resident) who was captured in 1969 and, as of 2016, is still in a tank at SeaWorld San Diego.

Fifty years after the harpooning of Moby Doll, Spong wrote in *Whalewatcher*, "In the long run, the whales will only be saved when we humans no longer regard them as resources to be exploited and 'managed,' but rather as fellow creatures—self-organized social animals—with clear rights that we acknowledge, grant, and protect. Paramount among these rights should be those that address issues of habitat protection and freedom."

Spong and Greenpeace didn't just change the world for whales; they changed the world for humans. As the Vancouver group exploded into a global phenomenon, it helped launch the idea of nongovernmental organizations as political players. Today, it's almost unthinkable to imagine a major issue that doesn't have at least one NGO leading the fight.

The most prominent NGO advocating for whales is the Sea Shepherd Conservation Society, founded in 1977 by Paul Watson after he was thrown out of Greenpeace for an approach that was less activist than outlaw. The Greenpeace model is Gandhi. Watson brands himself as an eco-pirate and proudly flies the Jolly Roger.

Bob Hunter was famous for turning to the I Ching for guidance, but Spong always looked to Skana. "She started it all," Weyler recalls Spong telling Hunter. "In case you wondered, we're working for

Skana. We're her ambassadors. She wants out, and wants her people to be free." But it wasn't Skana's playful intelligence that initially sparked Spong's interest in the killers he fights to call orcas. It was Moby Doll's brain.

WHEREAS SPONG OBSESSED over Moby's mind, John Ford became fascinated by the whale's voice. Ford, who met Moby Doll during the open house at the dry dock as a nine-year-old boy, landed a summer job at the Vancouver Aquarium after finishing his first year studying science at UBC. His mother was one of the docents—the aquarium's team of volunteer female tour guides—so Ford had an in on the ground floor. And that's where he started.

"I got a job as a floor boy—a popcorn sweeper after the whale show. My beat was the outside stands of the bleachers around the killer whale pool. So I spent a lot more time leaning on my broom and watching the whales than I did sweeping popcorn and cigarette butts." He says Newman used to regularly approach volunteers and staff and ask them, "What did you learn today?" Ford wanted to learn something, so every day that summer he watched Skana and Hyak and listened. "The next year, I got a position in the marine mammal department and started doing the beluga shows. Then the next year, I graduated to working with Skana and Hyak." Ford was a trainer for them for two years, and Newman urged the budding scientist to pursue his PhD.

As an undergrad, Ford studied orca acoustics and recorded whales with a hydrophone and tape recorder he borrowed from the Canadian navy—the same equipment Penfold and McGeer had used to record Moby. Ford worked with Dean Fisher, a professor in the zoology department at UBC, who had served on Moby's medical staff. "He was very interested in whales and whale sounds, and he actually had some recordings on old tapes that he let me borrow. There were miscellaneous tapes from the navy, and there was also a tape from Moby Doll. So I put that on the tape recorder, and I listened to it, and I was really struck at the sounds that were so strident and harsh and metallic in quality. They really are unusual sounds and a little bit sad in a way," says Ford. "This was recorded early on, when he was still not even in Jericho, and these calls were burnt into my acoustic memory."

Ford couldn't shake his fascination with whale calls and made them the subject of his PhD thesis. "It's pitch and time," he explains. "Some calls get highly elaborate." The work he studied included the paper produced by the Harvard duo Schevill and Watkins, based on their work with Moby. "They were first to describe echolocation in the species from their recordings at Jericho."

After spending years watching whales in captivity, Ford wanted to record wild whales and set out to meet the northern residents. Then, in the fall of 1978, he took a trip to the mouth of the Fraser River to record southern residents for the first time. "I put the hydrophone on the side of the boat, and I was recording the sounds, and they all sounded pretty alien to me, because the dialects are very different from the northern residents, which I had started becoming familiar with, and then, all of the sudden, in the middle of these calls, is the one I remembered so vividly from the Moby Doll tapes. I realized, in that moment, that this was the pod Moby Doll must have come from. It was J pod." Ford was hearing the sad voice that had haunted him— Moby's voice. Even to an untrained ear, modern J pod calls sound like the cries of Moby Doll.

Fifteen years after Sam Burich harpooned the young whale off East Point, Ford found Moby's family, perhaps even found the same whales who had lifted their pod member to the surface to keep him from drowning, the whale who stayed with Moby for the long journey to Vancouver and kept calling to him from the wild. The whales who visited the pen in Jericho the day Moby died. The discovery was a revelation. Ford hadn't just found Moby's family; because he recognized Moby's voice, he had discovered her language and evidence of orca culture.

"The whole notion of pod-specific dialect was totally new. There's no precedent in any other mammal," says Ford. "These calls out-live the whales, the individuals that make them. It's like an acoustic culture that's propagated across generations from old whale to young whale and so on. It's a fascinating thing. It was a wonderful moment out there in the boat when I recognized the sounds coming from J pod to be Moby Doll's signature sounds."

Ford's colleagues initially doubted his thesis that each pod had its own dialect, but he soon reframed the way the world saw whales by confirming how distinct the pods and ecotypes truly are. "The northern residents, where there are sixteen pods—there are three different clans with different language groups." How different? "They're like Swahili, versus English, versus Japanese." Twenty-five years after McGeer dreamed Moby Doll might reveal the secrets of a new language, Ford did just that. "Mike Bigg used to laugh and say I had no business even speculating that these things had different dialects at the family level. It was just through my ignorance that I proposed that. And then I went out and found they actually did have dialects at the family level, which surprised all of us."

The discovery also revealed that Moby came from "the most residential" of the resident pods. "The other groups, K and L pods, tend to leave the area for the winter; now we know they go as far as Monterey, California, sometimes up to the Haida Gwaii area. But J pod doesn't go quite as far and spends far more time in the Strait of Georgia. So it makes sense, in a way, that it would be J pod that Moby Doll was caught from," says Ford, "because it would be the one most likely to swim by East Point."

Through his acoustic research, Ford later confirmed that other members of J pod included the first Shamu. The more time Ford spent with the whales, the more he realized how rich their linguistic culture is.

We now know that killer whales are one of the very few mammalian species that can learn new sounds and reproduce them. Dogs and cats, for example—there's not a chance you could teach a dog to meow or a cat to bark. It's a very rare ability to learn sounds and reproduce them. We can do it, as humans. Some primates can. Some of the whales can. We know [with] humpback whales, for example, their song is learned; they mimic each other. Killer whales, we now know, grow up with a blank slate for "language," but they learn from their mother; very likely they may learn in the uterus, because sound travels perfectly through the body into the ears of a whale in utero. Anyway, they learn the family dialect, and that plays a role in giving them a kin identity badge, and that dialect sticks with them for life. So the calls Moby Doll made in 1964—we still hear today from his kin group that still exists out there.

CHAPTER FOURTEEN

THE WHALE WHO CHANGED THE WORLD

"Like religion, ecology seeks to answer the infinite mysteries of life itself. Harnessing the tools of logic, deduction, analysis, and empiricism, ecology may prove to be the first true science-religion."

BOB HUNTER, "GREENPEACE: DECLARATION OF INTERDEPENDENCE," 1976

I F ALL ROADS lead to Rome, all oceans lead to Moby Doll.

In the summer of 2013, forty-nine years after Moby Doll was harpooned, Newman and McGeer returned to Saturna Island, the place where killer whales became orcas and orcas became pets. Today, if you love whales, Saturna is considered one of the wonders of the world. McGeer visits the tiny island often—some of the three hundred full-time residents are relatives. For Newman, this was his first time on Saturna since the day he met Moby. And this weekend, the men were returning as conquering heroes.

In 2010, when the newly formed Saturna Island Heritage Committee began sharing local lore with tourists, the volunteer guides quickly discovered that the story that really captured the imagination of their visitors was Moby Doll's. As the fiftieth anniversary of the hunt approached, members of the community banded together to host a gathering of professional and amateur orca enthusiasts that they named the Moby Doll Orca Symposium: Reflections on Change.

They invited nearly a dozen experts to appear on panels, but the headliners were the leaders of the original Operation Killer Whale.

Arriving by floatplane—just as they had nearly fifty years earlier, when they flew out to meet a monster—Newman and McGeer pulled up at the Lyall Harbour dock, where they were greeted by their enthusiastic hosts.

Newman retired from the aquarium in 1993, but he kept diving for fun and for research. Now eighty-nine, Newman had only given up diving seven years earlier, after swimming with the fish off the shores of Maui, because his eyesight was vanishing as a result of macular degeneration. He was still writing research papers, articles, and books about a lifetime of aquatic adventures.

In 1996, the Vancouver Aquarium, the first place to introduce a killer whale to the world, became the first aquarium to declare it would no longer capture cetaceans in the wild. Five years later, the aquarium became one of the first to voluntarily stop displaying orcas, gifting their last captive, Bjossa, to SeaWorld. In 2013, the aquarium still housed a few cetaceans—belugas and dolphins—a subject of perpetual and passionate debate.

The Vancouver Aquarium has always been the site of passionate protests—from the handful of people campaigning to free Moby, such as Florence Barr and Maisie Hurley, to Spong lobbying to release Skana and everyone he and Greenpeace inspired. Canada's west coast is known for its commitment to the natural world, but it's also possible that by trying to mix research and entertainment, the aquarium inadvertently inspired their most passionate critics.

Newman suspected that his success in helping the public fall in love with Vancouver's whales inadvertently led to the vehement protests against captivity in Vancouver. From the moment Walter needed to be renamed, the public was invited to name almost everything at the aquarium that might become a box office draw. Since the aquarium's whales were treated as individuals, and staff shared the news of their pregnancies, miscarriages, and illnesses, the whale's lives were publicly celebrated and their deaths mourned as tragedies.

Newman believes this transparency led to a level of community investment in each animal that may have been unique to Vancouver.

Shamu was eternal. When a whale died at SeaWorld, he or she generally died offstage. There was only one Skana, only one Moby Doll. If Newman had followed SeaWorld's lead, Skana—or Moby Doll—might still be alive and well and swimming in a tank to amuse tourists. The aquarium staff would know they were displaying Skana the seventh or seventeenth, but the public would be collecting the same souvenirs that were on sale in the 1970s. Instead, when any of Newman's cetacean celebrities died, the aquarium shared the news. This practice may have been educational, but it was an invitation to outrage. Also, unlike SeaWorld—which relies on tourists—the Vancouver Aquarium primarily draws local visitors, who get to know and care for the individual creatures on display.

McGeer was still studying brains. He and Edith are among the world's foremost neuroscientists, famous for their research on concussions, Parkinson's, and Alzheimer's. Their lab is home to one of the world's most extensive collections of human brains—more than eight hundred. McGeer served in the B.C. provincial government until 1986, spending nearly a decade as a cabinet minister, including a stint as B.C.'s first minister of universities, science and communications. Although Moby's brain vanished from the lab (courtesy of Spong, who says he no longer knows its whereabouts), McGeer still owns a scale model.

Bauer was invited to the conference too, and had agreed to lead a tour of East Point. It wasn't until the last passenger stepped off the final ferry to Saturna the night before the event that the disappointed hosts realized he wasn't going to attend. Whereas Newman and McGeer were enthusiastic about the reunion, the shy Bauer, who had almost never spoken publicly about his experiences with Moby, was skittish.

Bauer, who now sports a white beard that would make Burich proud, explains that he skipped the symposium in part because he was concerned his version of events might have contradicted the mentor he still calls "Dr. Newman." Newman's biography—and many interviews—referred to Moby being "towed" to Vancouver. Bauer is adamant that he and Burich never stopped watching their captive to make sure they didn't injure the whale any further than they already had once the decision was made to save him. "We never towed Moby—we led him," says Bauer, "like a puppy on a leash."

Bauer also worried that it might be awkward if he told the audience about declaring Moby a male at the same time he had told Burich the whale could be saved. Bauer says he screened his footage of the capture for the aquarium board back in 1965 and was asked to destroy the film. Bauer didn't destroy it, but in deference to his mentors, he never showed it again. He says that once the public fell in love with whales—and Namu became a superstar—Newman and the aquarium board weren't keen on shining a spotlight on the way Moby was caught.

In 2010, Bauer was appointed as an adjunct professor at UBC. The man identified for almost fifty years in Moby lore as "an amateur ichthyologist" was now a professional ichthyologist, teaching students about fisheries and fishing at the same place he had met his original mentors.

Sam Burich died in 1989. He remained friends with Bauer—and the Fletchers—long after the expedition had ended. While Burich was working on the aquarium's model, he sculpted a gift for Bauer as a memory of their adventures. The two were meeting for dinner when Burich presented Bauer with his first anatomically correct sculpture of Moby, or at least part of Moby—his penis. It was the perfect gift. After being dismissed by the "experts," Bauer felt vindicated. The sculpture of Moby's dick is still at Bauer's house—a prize possession.

The full-sized, anatomically accurate replica of the orca that Newman commissioned is in storage and in serious need of repairs and a new coat of paint—a faded relic from a bygone age.

The whales who rescued Moby were never identified—but Bauer's footage and photos might one day solve that mystery.

At the conference on Saturna, Vancouver Aquarium officials presented their hosts with Moby's skull. After forty-nine years, the whale was finally home. They also offered to deliver Burich's original sculpture, but the life-sized replica was almost the size of the island's museum.

Newman and McGeer started the morning onstage in Saturna's recreation center, where they called for an end to all whaling and a one-year moratorium on herring fishing so that the salmon population could recover enough to feed the orcas. McGeer was, as usual, the more vehement. The 220 people crowding the community hall—roughly 150 of them orca experts from off island—applauded as the elders preached conservation.

Architect Richard Blagborne, chairman of Saturna's Heritage Committee, had been the driving force behind organizing the symposium and convincing Newman and McGeer to attend. He'd also spent months wooing Bauer. Blagborne hoped the event would lure the people he referred to as "orcaholics" to the island to promote the idea of "terrestrial whale watching"—watching orcas and other whales from shore. His dream is to turn Saturna into a safe haven for whales—an appropriate legacy for Newman, McGeer, and Moby. "The whales come so close, and they come by quite regularly in the summer, so it's a terrific thrill to be there and have the whales come to you, rather than going and chasing them in boats." Blagborne's plan is to use Moby's story to convince government officials to turn the waters around Saturna into an international marine sanctuary, possibly a Canadian Heritage site and, ideally, a World Heritage site. He hopes that this will ultimately protect orcas not just from threats such as pollution but also from the people who love them—including whale watchers. A lack of boats also means a lack of sounds interfering with the acoustic environment. Blagborne and his fellow organizers hoped showing off Saturna would convince the world's top orca experts to support their cause.

McGeer and Newman loved the idea that Saturna would be recognized for its role in human and orca history. "I think Saturna

Island is going to become world famous, because it changed attitudes towards whales and whaling," says McGeer. "It's my hope that whaling will be given up altogether. I don't see any reason for continuing it. And maybe Saturna Island will be the focus that will make that happen."

One of the other speakers was John Ford. In 2001, Ford joined Fisheries and Oceans Canada as head of their Cetacean Research Program at the Pacific Biological Station in Nanaimo—the position once held by Gordon Pike, one of the original members of Operation Killer Whale. Ford is also an adjunct professor in UBC's Department of Zoology.

Dr. Peter Ross, Canada's leading marine mammal toxicologist, warned the audience that toxins in the water weren't disappearing quickly enough. Courtesy of the remnants of PCBs, which had been outlawed decades earlier, and exposure to other persistent organic pollutants (POPs), not only through the food they eat but through toxins in and on the water, the southern residents are among the most contaminated marine mammals on the planet. Bigg's whales are the most PCB-contaminated marine mammals in the world. How toxic? Toxic enough that in the U.S. some killer whales have been treated as chemical waste. In Canada, the only reason the more contaminated orcas don't qualify as hazardous waste is because regulations only apply to man-made products.

Ross warned that in recent years, dead whales were turning up poisoned, and live ones were unable to give birth. One male whale's genitals never fully developed. A female whale and her calf both died after an agonizing childbirth because the mother was unable to expel her baby. Not long after the symposium, another young killer was delivered with other whales assisting with the birth, pulling the calf out of the mother with their teeth. Ross blames the chemicals for wreaking havoc with the orcas' hormones and is quick to point out that this is the same water humans are getting fish from. The research Ross was doing was so depressing—and probably so damaging to the case for increased tanker traffic on the West Coast—that he was one of numerous Canadian scientists muzzled and then fired by Prime Minister Stephen Harper's Conservative government. The Vancouver Aquarium put Ross on staff so that he could continue his research.

Asked why we should care about the fate of these creatures, most scientists at the symposium offered the same warning—often using the same phrase—describing killer whales as "the canary in the coal mine." Their argument for saving the whales: if these massive canaries can't survive, neither will we. Says Ford, "If we can ensure the survival and prosperity of killer whales on this coast, we can be certain that the underlying marine ecosystem is being preserved."

If we can't...

In addition to concerns about the garbage being dumped into the water, Ford warned that whales are being traumatized by acoustic pollution. Boats are making it harder for orcas to hear each other. Humans who are disturbed by noise have forced airplanes and cars to muffle their engines, but whales don't have lobby groups pushing legislators to force boats to use quieter motors. A new threat on the acoustic front is fish farms using sonic devices to scare off seals and sea lions that are also disorienting whales.

All the noise in the ocean is causing what Ford describes as the "cocktail party effect," in which killer whales and other sea creatures have had to increase the volume of their calls to cut through the human-made cacophony. The noise and number of boats on the water has also made it difficult for whales to sleep, especially since they are perpetually being chased by an endless stream of podparazzi. And whale watching is a growth industry; the southern resident killer whales are believed to generate roughly $70 million a year for the Washington State economy, and the Pacific Whale Watch Association had thirty-six operators in Washington and B.C. in 2014—responsible for nearly fifteen thousand trips a year, with roughly 400,000 whale watchers on board.

Michael Bigg's name came up frequently throughout the day, and when whale lovers mentioned him, they'd get a dreamy look in their eyes, as if he were the Orca Lama. A few years earlier, whale researchers acknowledged Bigg's groundbreaking work by renaming transients Bigg's whales in his honor. Bigg's work led to the discovery of other ecotypes as well—most recently, a new group of killer whales in the Salish Sea known as offshores, believed to survive on a diet of sleeper sharks. Orcas in other parts of the world have different designations, and there are now ten recognized ecotypes that break down along similar lines to Bigg's original identifications of mammal eaters and fish eaters—and in all cases, the diets can be quite specialized. A group of mammal eaters in California's favorite feast is gray whale. A clan of residents in New Zealand survives almost entirely on rays, sometimes working in teams to pluck the stinger.

In their closing remarks at the symposium, Newman and McGeer urged the people of Saturna to promote their island as the place where the world's view of whales shifted and to embrace terrestrial whale watching. Moby's relatives, they said, could be seen from shore instead of being trapped in tanks or chased as if they were being hunted by a pack of hound dogs. The people who had changed the way we see whales wanted to change the way we watch them.

In 1964, no one was watching whales for fun. Today, every orca in the Salish Sea is a star. It began with the census started by Bigg, which is now the longest continuously running annual survey of a population of any species of whale in the world, and since the 1980s, Kenneth Balcomb has been the man in charge. Balcomb might be the world's ultimate whale watcher. He and his team take pictures of every whale on the Salish Sea every time they're close enough to spot. The result is that scientists know more about these whales than any other population of marine mammals in the world. And sharing that research has made North America's west coast whales even more famous.

There are websites and Twitter feeds dedicated to following the travels of the southern residents. Every orca in J, K, and L pods has his or her own Facebook fanpage. Technological advancements have led to even more elaborate tracking, and orcas in the Salish

Sea and around the world are being filmed and photographed by both illegal and officially sanctioned drones. Research organizations, including the Canadian government, have listening stations in the Salish Sea to record the whales' conversations. In 2016, several groups on both sides of the border decided to start sharing data to create a medical database for the local orcas. The oceans may be almost endless, but because these creatures don't stray outside their ancient boundaries, their home has become a very large fishbowl. Once you include Granny and the original Shamu in the mix—and their guest-starring role as the lead orca's family in the opening and closing credits of *Free Willy*—the southern residents are the most photographed, filmed, recorded, and documented mammals on the planet who aren't either running a country or headlining Hollywood blockbusters.

The stories of these whales have changed the narrative around the world. The campaigns against orca captures and captivity that were spearheaded in Washington and British Columbia have spread worldwide. No one is using whales for target practice, but killer whales located in Russian waters are still being captured for marine displays in Russia and China, with the Russian government issuing hunting permits to a new—and hopefully final—generation of orca cowboys.

Erich Hoyt, author of numerous books about whales and founder and co-director of the Far East Russia Orca Project (FEROP), which is currently studying orcas and other whales throughout Russian Pacific waters, warns that

> as we speak, Russian orcas are now being captured and some killed in the process in a situation that recalls what happened to the southern and northern communities of orcas in the Pacific Northwest 40 to 50 years ago. Once again, captors who smell big dollars to be made are taking killer whales from a population that is not fully studied or understood. So far at least nine orcas have been sent to China and three are on display in Moscow, with more in holding

pens in Vladivostok. So vote with your feet when it comes to orcas in captivity. Stay away from all aquariums that exhibit whales and dolphins, or if you do go, let them know clearly but politely that you disagree with this aspect of their facility.

Hoyt says that in Russia, where killer whale shows are a new phenomenon, there is already some public opposition to the displays, but in Japan, protests have been limited. "Most of what you see has been foreigners and a few Japanese protesting Taiji drive hunting. I do know Japanese people who oppose capturing killer whales and keeping them in Japanese aquariums, but the feelings about cetaceans in captivity in Asia, which includes Japan, are generally not at all like what it is in North America, South America, and Europe. For Asia, India is an exception where they have outlawed captivity of cetaceans in the last five years or so, although they have never had an orca being displayed in India."

ALMOST EVERYONE AT the symposium knew the story of Moby Doll—or at least thought they did—even before they arrived. But it was more likely they knew the legend, because even the most reliable sources of orca history tended to be unclear on a few of the facts or ignored the facts for a better story. Like they say in the movie *The Man Who Shot Liberty Valance*, "When the legend becomes fact, print the legend."

From the moment Moby was hooked, the story shifted daily, depending on who was telling it. The "monster" ranged from fifteen to twenty feet long and weighed between six thousand and fifteen thousand pounds. It was tethered to the boat on a length of rope that was two hundred, four hundred, or six hundred feet long. The pole used to hold the four-inch syringe to administer antibiotics was reported as eight, ten, or twelve feet. The stay at the dry dock cost the owner either $1,000 a day or $15,000 a day. And over fifty years, the myths multiplied.

Among the most common Moby myths, some of which sprang up while the whale was still alive, are:

The whale was intentionally captured by the aquarium.

The whale was exhibited at the aquarium.

The whale didn't eat, because the naïve scientists had no idea what to feed it.

The whale was on constant display to the public until its death. This usually includes the claim that admission was charged. A common variation on this theme is that the aquarium made big bucks at the box office from people paying to see Moby.

So many stories over the last fifty years have mocked the aquarium experts for accidentally starving the whale by trying to tempt Moby with all the wrong foods that even Newman and McGeer forgot that the first dish they tried to serve their whale was salmon. It was only after Moby turned up his nose at the salmon that they attempted the more exotic meals that scientists, books, and fishermen claimed would appeal to their captive. Killer whales were being shot on sight for eating salmon—of course Newman and McGeer knew it was a favorite food.

Many reports ridicule the idea of tempting Moby with blubber and whale tongues, suggesting that this kind of cannibalism was unheard of among orcas. The meal would be as repulsive, or perplexing, to a resident whale like Moby as a slice of pizza, but killer whales earned their name and reputation by eating other whales. Bigg's whales and other mammal-eating orcas might not be keen on blubber, but they are happy to feast on the tongue and lips of other types of whales.

One popular Moby "fact" is that the duke and duchess of Westminster had a private audience with the whale. This event was featured in a lengthy story in *Reader's Digest*, originally published in *Rod & Gun*. The duke and duchess were in Vancouver, but there's no mention of anyone escorting them into the enclosure at Jericho. Newman, McGeer, McLeod, and Bauer have no memory of a royal visit. Some authors upgraded the duke and duchess of Westminster to the duke and duchess of Windsor. But barring a secret mission worthy of James Bond, it appears the only way visiting royals met Moby was through the media of the day.

The *Reader's Digest* story also stated that the London *Times* reported Moby's death in the same headline size that announced the end of World War II. The *Times* obituary for Moby was substantial, but the headline wasn't especially large—and the story ran on page eleven.

Perhaps the most confusing bit of Moby lore is that the whale received its name courtesy of a contest on a Vancouver radio station. Newman refers to the contest in his autobiography but offers no details about it, and the 1964 Vancouver Aquarium newsletters (likely written by Newman) offer only a single-line reference to a contest that includes no mention of any names that were submitted for consideration or any contestants. Newman, Bauer, and McLeod couldn't remember any details about a naming contest, though McGeer recalls the name being discussed in an informal poll by an on-air host and developing "a huge radio following." So there may have been a radio poll, but if there was a "contest" to come up with the name, it seems likely that the winner was Newman. As a consummate showman and master of staying in the limelight while sharing it with others, Newman most certainly would have publicly celebrated whoever named Moby. That's how the aquarium handled future competitions. Less than a year after Moby's death, the *Vancouver Sun* reported that a toy company that was making little Moby Doll dolls was trying to claim the trademark to the name, which could prevent the aquarium from using it. The company ultimately won the rights to the name–but their trademark was limited to "toys only, namely, toy whales." The *Sun* coverage noted that Newman "coined" the name Moby Doll.

Names have power. Names have magic in them.

Today, McGeer echoes the philosophy of the young scientist he'd hired—Paul Spong—and believes it's time to stop referring to Moby Doll's species as "killer whales." Says McGeer, "Call them orcas!"

Regardless of how scientists may feel about respecting the history of the name, there's no world in which "killer" sounds like a safe species to swim with. If you're on their menu, the name is accurate, but if you're not—and we're clearly not—it's an archaic holdover from an ancient era that makes it harder to save this vital species.

Charlotte Epstein, an assistant professor in the Department of Government and International Relations at the University of Sydney, was trying to figure out how whales went from monsters to Muppets when she came across the story of Moby Doll.

Epstein believes the moment Newman dubbed his whale Moby Doll, he reframed the way we saw the species. "Suddenly Moby Doll becomes a doll, a cuddly toy. It becomes something you give to kids, whereas Moby Dick was not something that was cute or that you would have wanted to bring to a kiddie's room—except as a very scary story about how dangerous nature can be and how powerful nature can be." Moby's capture and, more significantly, Moby's name changed human—and cetacean—history.

When Ken Balcomb helped transform J2 into "Granny," he made it easier for the media and the public not only to identify with wild orcas but also to fall in love with them. And it's hard to imagine a hit movie called *Free J2*.

In the mid-1990s, environmentalists in B.C. decided to save a remote, unnamed rainforest that loggers referred to as TimberWest cutblock 11-370. The activists started by renaming the area they wanted to protect and created the Great Bear Rainforest. It would have been tough to find a few dozen people willing to rescue a cutblock—but the world fell in love with the Great Bear Rainforest. The Great Bear had previously been known as the Kermode bear, which didn't make headlines that often until it started being referred to as the spirit bear. How could even the most heartless capitalist argue that it was necessary to log the home of the spirit bear? Now environmentalists are referring to the water around the forest as the Great Bear Sea. If the maple, spruce, and fir were named Flopsy, Mopsy, and Cottontail, that might be the end of logging. Perhaps it's time for a section of the Salish Sea to become the Great Whale Watershed or the Moby Doll Marine Sanctuary.

AFTER NEWMAN AND McGeer regaled the audience at the symposium, everyone took a field trip to East Point to discover where it all began. While most people strolled down the path towards the ocean to see where Burich had fired the harpoon, Newman slowly walked up the grassy hill to the East Point light. The aquarium's senior vice-president and general manager, Clint Wright, held Newman's elbow to help his friend navigate the gentle slope a stone's throw from the treacherous Boiling Reef. As he approached the cliff edge, Newman gazed out at the water, his eyes glassy from macular degeneration, and tried to picture the scene from fifty years ago, superimposed over a landscape backdropped by an oil refinery and a coal container facility in Washington State.

Standing a few hundred yards from where Bauer had spotted Moby's pod, Newman squinted through his thick dark glasses, looking out at the open ocean. "It's wonderful," he said with a laugh. "It's like seeing a memory of your childhood, although I wasn't very young. I was forty."

It seemed everything had changed since the days Newman was picturing. The light was still there, but the last lighthouse keeper left in 1996, and the beacon was now automated. The seventy-year-old Fog Alarm Building had been decommissioned in the early 1990s and in 2010 was reopened as Saturna's museum. Both the light and fog alarm were granted historic protected status—in part because of their connection to the story of Moby Doll.

Even the water Newman was peering at had a different name—the Salish Sea.

That sea is now a tanker route, and the greatest dangers to whales in the wild today aren't would-be Barnums or Griffins or Newmans but loss of habitat and food.

And the number one threat to whales today?

"Humans," Newman answered without hesitation. "When my great-grandfather was born, there were 1 billion people on the earth. When I was born, there were 2 billion. Fifty years ago, there were 3 billion. Now, there are over 7 billion. And thirty years from now, there are going to be 10 billion. And the insatiable needs of humans is a serious problem for most big animals. What should we do about it?

It's very hard for governments to set aside significant protected areas. But if the world is going to have elephants, for example, or whales, there have to be large protected areas." Newman hoped the waters around Saturna would be one of those areas. "When you go to Africa, you want to see the lions on the Serengeti, and when you come to British Columbia, you want to see the killer whale."

Newman wasn't convinced that Moby's capture changed the world for whales, though he was proud that it changed the perception of them. "I think along the coast of western Canada, for example, there's an appreciation for killer whales that did not exist. Moby Doll stimulated the interest for collecting live whales, and then this became our problem. Thinking about East Point and our little operation there, it was astounding how this activity on Saturna Island could have had such an impact all over the place. But it hasn't changed the whole world, because we still have the problem of whaling in certain places." Newman expressed his frustration about how the Japanese whaling industry continues to kill whales—allegedly to conduct scientific research before conveniently selling their specimens as food. Other nations such as Norway and Iceland also maintain an active whaling industry. Then Newman talked about the importance of the anti-whaling campaigns being conducted by Paul Watson and the Sea Shepherd Society.

McGeer was, as always, more effusive. "People had considered this the most fearsome creature on the planet. The most vicious. The most predatory. Without any rivals. It could beat anything in the oceans, so, therefore, it qualified as the most feared of all beasts. Totally wrong. So I guess Moby Doll changed the world's attitudes towards killer whales. Now they're protected; now you're not allowed to go near them."

Moby's most profound legacy was in the people he inspired.

Without Moby, Michael Bigg probably would have stuck to studying seals, and we might never have known it was possible to identify individual whales on sight or how few killer whales there were until it was too late to save them.

John Ford would never have memorized a whale's calls, and we wouldn't know that each pod has their own unique dialect and culture.

Paul Spong would have stuck to studying human brains, and Greenpeace would be a footnote from the 1970s—a long-forgotten collection of antinuke hippies almost no one outside of Vancouver ever would have heard of. Without Spong inspiring the original Greenpeace campaigns against Russian whalers, would anyone have stepped up to save the whales?

In his eulogy for Greenpeace founder Bob Hunter, Watson said, "If ecology becomes the religion of the future—as I believe it will— Bob Hunter will be known as our ecological Messiah."

Was Hunter the Messiah? Or was he the first prophet of the gospel of Moby Doll—the Christ Whale who taught blind men to see at Jericho, then died to save his species?

The first disciples were the men who caught Moby, ignoring everything the textbooks told them about how dangerous these creatures were and keeping the whale alive—even when they believed he might kill them.

Nearly nine hundred whales from various species were killed commercially in B.C. in 1964—and it's impossible to know how many killer whales were shot on sight for the crime of eating salmon. Nobody protested. Nobody cared. Then Moby Doll arrived in Vancouver and everything changed. Moby was the last killer whale and the first orca.

Even the fact that Moby was a resident had a huge impact on the way his species was perceived. If Moby was a mammal eater and had skinned a seal or feasted on whale tongue, that would have confirmed everyone's worst nightmares about the apex predators. Instead of seeing a killer—a savage monster like Moby Dick—the world met a cuddly companion, Moby Doll. Just as Spong stopped referring to the whales as killers, so did the media and the public. And thanks to that $20,000 price tag Newman placed on his prize, fishermen stopped seeing a worthless pest that ate their food and started seeing dollar signs. So did potential exhibitors. The story of Moby Doll became the story of Namu and Shamu and all the other killer whales who were transformed into unwilling circus performers.

Because those first captive orcas became the ambassadors and icons of the species, the public now thinks that all whales are as social, intelligent, and endangered as the southern residents. When research revealed that some species, like humpbacks, were no longer endangered—at least in some areas—anti-whaling arguments shifted from the realm of science and conservation to ethics and philosophy. Instead of rallying against the threat of extinction, protestors focused on the intelligence, personality, and majesty of the whales. The argument was no longer that we should avoid killing off the last of the species but that whales deserve to live because they're whales.

For a long time, humans have wondered about the possibility of intelligent life on other planets while ignoring the intelligent life on this one.

The idea of viewing orcas as our equals instead of creatures we have "dominion over" has implications beyond religion. Today's most compelling monkey trials aren't about evolution but about whether monkeys should be recognized as nonhuman persons—and the same case is being made for cetaceans by groups like the Kimmela Center for Animal Advocacy, which is leading the fight for nonhuman rights. Orcas have a language and a culture that predates ours, so how do we justify imprisoning them or, more importantly, destroying their habitat? Orcas may not need the right to vote, but if they are declared "persons," then it becomes difficult to argue that human rights supersede their rights—and orcas still live in every ocean on the planet.

That's why the ripple effect of granting any rights to orcas has the potential to become a tidal wave. If orcas have the right to a safe environment, do we still have the right to steer tankers through their feeding areas?

If orcas have the right to eat, do we still get first dibs on all the fish?

In 2010, the United Nations declared clean water "a fundamental human right." If that same right applies to orcas, everything changes.

At the annual meeting of the American Association for the Advancement of Science in Vancouver in 2012—an event described as the world's largest science conference—researchers presented the "Declaration of Rights for Cetaceans: Whales and Dolphins," which was drafted in Helsinki two years earlier. The declaration opens with a preamble that begins, "Based on the principle of the equal treatment of all persons."

The legal concept of "personhood" has been used to prevent women, minorities, and children from being treated as property and has led to all humans being treated as equals (at least in theory) to the white men running the world. It's also the crux of legal challenges to abortion—the moment a fetus becomes a person, it has rights.

For animal rights activists, the argument that a fetus could have rights opens the door to the definition of "person." Most animal rights court cases to date have focused on captivity—and representatives of several species in various countries have won some kind of "emancipated" status—but the captivity debate is just the tip of the orca iceberg. The issue with more complicated and extensive implications for their species and ours isn't how we treat the handful of orcas stuck in fish tanks but how we treat the habitat of whales in the wild.

It's tough enough to argue that gorillas who can sign enough words to get decent grades in high school shouldn't be accorded the same basic rights as a human. But what is the basis for claiming that a compassionate, social, and intelligent species with its own language, culture, and history isn't entitled to live in peace? The economic justification for treating orcas like any other fish in the sea is obvious—but what's the moral justification?

The will, the passion, and even the money to fight for orcas and other cetaceans exists. The challenge is picking battles worth fighting. In 1988, three countries spent an estimated $1 million to save three humpbacks trapped in the ice in Barrow, Alaska. Freeing the real Willy—or Keiko, the whale who inspired Willy—and attempting to reunite him with his pod in Iceland was estimated to cost a block-buster sum of nearly $20 million. Armchair activists outraged by the anti-captivity movie *Blackfish* put massive amounts of time, money, and energy into attacking SeaWorld. Musicians canceled concerts at the marine parks, and tourists stayed away in droves. In 2016, Sea-World promised that they would finally stop breeding new Shamus, and activists and the media turned their spotlight on the fate of their twentysomething captive whales.

But what if a fraction of that time, money, and energy were devoted to a campaign to knock down some of the dams in Washington State that are doing virtually nothing for the economy except killing the salmon that feed the orcas? Or to fighting to close the Pacific herring fishery for a year to allow the salmon stocks to recover? Or to battling against the ubiquitous use of a toxic flame retardant that was added to furniture because tobacco lobbyists found a way to blame couches and cribs for causing fires started by cigarettes? Or to supporting any legal case that could lead to more rights for orcas? What if the musicians who canceled their concerts at SeaWorld held fundraisers for nonhuman rights or to fund campaigns designed to replenish the salmon stocks?

It would be tragic if Lolita, who was taken from L pod at Penn Cove, Washington, in 1970, or Corky, the orca Spong has spent decades lobbying to return to A5 pod after being held in captivity since 1969, never saw the open ocean again—but it would be a crime against nature and humanity if there was no A5 pod or L pod for Corky and Lolita to return to. Alaskan orcas have never recovered from the *Exxon Valdez* oil spill in 1989, and one transient pod that was decimated by the spill is probably doomed. Today, the southern residents are potentially one tanker accident away from the nightmare extinction scenario that helped spark Newman's original hunt, where the only way any of these orcas will survive is if they're rescued from their home in the Salish Sea.

If orcas have rights, then these are no longer "our oceans" to pollute as we please, and the fish we're chasing to supply our sushi cravings are no longer "our salmon" or "our herring." Granting great apes or elephants personhood status might have an impact on the few parts of the planet where these species are found—and create headaches for zookeepers everywhere—but declaring orcas our equals would open a huge bucket of plankton. According orcas rights—almost any rights—would realign the rules of the planet so that the orcas truly would become the chiefs of the undersea world.

TODAY, ALMOST NOBODY can imagine shooting an orca—nevermind attacking a pod with bombs and bazookas. The biggest dangers have shifted from humans with rifles and machine guns to humans with tankers, toxins, and cameras. Climate change is altering everyone's habitat. And the oceans people once believed were infinite aren't deep enough to hide all our garbage.

With the discovery of gyres—swirling islands of decomposing plastic—in every ocean, Marshall McLuhan's global village found an aquatic equivalent. The seven seas are a global sewer. Nothing humans throw away disappears, because there is no "away." And sea creatures at the top of the food chain—especially the ocean's apex predators—are becoming increasingly toxic. There is now more plastic in the Pacific Ocean than plankton. The water near the gyres is so polluted that the fish and birds that live near them—there's no polite way to say this—shit plastic. Some scientists believe the Pacific gyre is bigger than the continental U.S., and there's a second gyre in the Atlantic about the same size. Our plastic is not going away. And neither are the chemicals we flush without a second thought. Perhaps, if orcas are given rights, we'll be forced to protect their environment, which means finally protecting our own. As Paul Watson says, "If the oceans die, we die."

For more than fifty years, the black-and-white patterns on orcas have been an environmental Rorschach test.

Fishermen saw blackfish—competitors, predators, danger.

Ted Griffin saw a childhood dream—and a financial windfall.

Michael Bigg saw something more compelling than seals and sea lions—an intelligent, endangered species.

John Ford heard something no one else could.

Paul Spong saw a creature who could outsmart humans.

Joe Bauer saw an animal worth risking his life for.

Sam Burich saw something terrifying and then, after firing his harpoon, a friend.

Pat McGeer saw an amazing brain.

Murray Newman saw "the most magnificent of all living creatures" and the ultimate aquarium specimen.

But until Moby Doll arrived in Vancouver, almost everyone who spotted those black-and-white swirls saw a monster. Today, we see an orca.

EPILOGUE

CAPTAIN AHAB CHASED Moby Dick for less than three years. I've chased Moby Doll for twenty. In 1996, I was researching a story about the Vancouver Aquarium and the latest skirmish in B.C.'s never-ending battle over cetaceans in captivity. At the time, there were two orcas in the aquarium, and I called the world's most infamous whale warrior, Paul Watson, for an inflammatory quote about why they should be set free.

When I reached Watson on the phone, I was surprised that he wasn't passionate about freeing whales who were already in captivity and that he didn't bash the aquarium. He surprised me again when he talked about sneaking into the whale pool and swimming with Skana. Then he shocked me with the news that the Vancouver Aquarium was the first place to ever capture and display a killer whale. And they didn't just catch it; they'd tried to kill it. Because the world is impossibly small, Watson first heard about Moby from one of his college professors—Kathy Newman. Watson threw the harpoon, and I was hooked. I had to find out what kind of monster would try to kill a lovable orca. I also began to wonder what the connection was between Vancouver being home to the first killer whale ever displayed in captivity and being the birthplace of Greenpeace and the Sea Shepherd. People kept telling me it was a coincidence, but it sure seemed like a pretty big coincidence.

Like everyone I know who grew up in Vancouver, I've always loved whales. Skana, the first whale Watson met, arrived in Stanley

Park in 1967, when I was five—just three years after Moby was caught. I'm sure my mom took my brother, David, and me there that first year. Everyone went. I don't remember much about meeting Skana when I was a kid, except that I loved her.

David and I always wanted to sit in the splash zone and wished we could feed the whales and pet them like the trainers did. If we could have jumped into the pool, we wouldn't have hesitated. Everybody knew that whales were smart and loveable and that they'd never hurt you. Whenever we traveled to big cities, we always wanted to visit their aquariums—especially if they had orcas.

As I visited Skana over the years, I started worrying that her tank was too small. I wished she had more room to swim. But I was always more concerned about the whales in the oceans than the ones in aquariums. I knew Greenpeace and the Sea Shepherd were doing God's work, and anyone who killed whales deserved their own circle of hell, spending eternity bouncing on the bottlenose of a dolphin.

Not long after talking to Watson, I contacted Newman and asked if he'd tell me about Moby Doll. He invited me to the house he'd shared with Kathy since the early 1960s, a wood-frame bungalow in West Vancouver. Naturally, it was near the ocean—the perfect habitat for humans. He didn't look like Ahab. He looked like an elderly academic. In any age, in any universe, Newman would look like an academic, but I soon discovered he was also an active diver, still traveling the world with Kathy to study new species.

The Newmans sat me down on their living room couch and offered me tea and cookies. Murray's eyes lit up as he told me how Moby Doll changed everything for him, the aquarium, the whales, and the world. Then he told me about the Canadian government's slaughter of the basking sharks, the bounties on sea lions, and the machine gun that was mounted to massacre orcas. He wanted to catch a killer whale, while we still had killer whales. But I had to know why Newman—why anyone—would think orcas were dangerous, why he'd send men out to kill one with a harpoon. He picked up a faded hardcover book published in 1963—Killer Whale!—opened it, and read a description of whales that sounded like a scene from *Jaws*. As Newman told me what everyone knew about orcas before his expedition, I realized that when he and his hunters made their individual decisions to save Moby, they believed they were risking their lives.

I had to fight past my love for whales and try to imagine what Burich saw when Moby surfaced. Instead of picturing a whale, I imagined "first contact" with an alien—and until E.T. appeared in 1982, that never ended well for the stranger from another planet. And I thought, somebody has to capture Newman's memories while he's still lucid enough to share them. I didn't care if that someone was me, but someone had to tell the story about how we went from using orcas for target practice to loving them to death.

In 1996, Newman was keen to share his whale tale, and I pitched it everywhere. But at the height of *Free Willy* mania—the movie about freeing a lovable orca that had become a phenomenon two years earlier—no one wanted to publish it. I tried to argue that without Moby Doll, there would have been no Willy to free and we might have finished off the last orca a decade ago with a side of wasabi. No sale. I even tried to sell the story as a documentary, despite having no clue how to make one. Potential producers were interested; broadcasters and funding agencies weren't.

Newman and I kept in touch. I remained fascinated by his story, and he liked the idea of someone telling it. Murray and Kathy sent me the occasional postcard from their diving adventures, along with a gift subscription to the diving magazine he wrote for. We also exchanged letters and, later, emails.

In 2007, I decided to hire someone to film Newman. I still didn't have a plan. I just thought someone needed to get his story on camera while he was still able to share it. After more than ten years of chasing Moby, ten years of talking about interviewing Newman "some day," it was finally happening. I'd arranged to hire a cameraman on my nickel when I received a letter from Newman informing me that he wasn't interested in talking about Moby anymore. He wrote to tell me that he wanted to "let the old whale rest in peace."

By this time, there were plenty of stories that mentioned Moby Doll. They were all about whales in captivity, and Newman was tired of being painted as the villain who had ushered in the age of Shamu. I knew that the other stories started from the same place I had—a post-Willy world where everybody knew that whales were social, loveable, and smarter than humans, since they lived in oceanfront property without jobs or mortgages.

I kept in contact with Newman, kept hoping that one day he'd change his mind. Finally, he did. In the summer of 2013, Newman invited me for lunch, and I arranged to film our meeting. The night before our scheduled visit, I received an email. I was afraid Newman was canceling again. Instead, he'd invited some old friends for lunch to share their Moby memories with me—including Pat McGeer, Gil Hewlett, and Chris Angus.

As the gang arrived at his home, one thing was abundantly clear—they loved this guy. They all shared variations on the same story—how they joined the aquarium after Newman convinced them that whatever he was doing couldn't possibly succeed without their help. Newman spoke a little more slowly than he had nearly twenty years earlier—but only a little. There were a few more catches in his speech, but he still rattled off names, dates, and details like he was reading them off his day-timer.

Angus was the first person I met who shared the idea of Moby as an orca ambassador—a concept I've heard since from numerous whale lovers. As a lifelong sci-fi buff, I loved the image of interspecies diplomacy. "Moby changed the world's attitude toward killer whales completely, absolutely completely," Angus told me. "Without those initial ambassadors for the species, I do believe the species would be vastly reduced in the oceans, because people wouldn't have the respect or the compassion for them that they have now." Angus described exactly what had captured my imagination at that first meeting with Newman—the idea of first contact.

I was eating tuna sandwiches with Newman and his crew when I found out I wasn't the only person who wanted to get the whole story from the sea horse's mouth. So did Richard Blagborne. That's when Newman mentioned the Saturna symposium.

A few minutes before Newman and McGeer stepped onstage to start the symposium, Lance Barrett-Lennard pulled up to the town hall in a fire engine–red Vancouver Aquarium van and flipped open the trunk. Inside was a box holding the remains of the guest of honor. Barrett-Lennard was delivering Moby's skull.

I asked if I could touch the remains of the whale who had changed the way we thought about whales. The monster's skull weighed almost nothing. It was fragile. Tiny. Of course it was tiny. It was small enough that in 1964 the scientists believed the whale was two years old. Just like I was.

The head of the aquarium's cetacean research program allowed me to help carry Moby into the hall. The skull was going to be displayed at the event before being secured in a transparent display case in Saturna's museum.

The summer after the visit to Saturna, Newman and McGeer decided to celebrate the fiftieth anniversary of Moby's capture with a lunch together at the aquarium. They invited me to join them. Naturally, the aquarium was in the midst of another controversy about captive cetaceans, with protesters lobbying to free the belugas. I received an email from McGeer a few nights before the lunch to tell me it had been canceled. The director of the aquarium had asked Newman and McGeer to postpone their meeting because of fears they might be spotted and exploited by opponents of the aquarium's policies.

Not long after the canceled lunch, I finally met Joe Bauer at a cafe in Steveston—the fishing village near Vancouver he's always called home. The cafe is a place where old fishermen gather to swap stories, but Bauer was wary of sharing his memories with me—in part because he worried they might contradict Newman's. The baby of the expedition was now a seventy-seven-year-old graybeard wearing a carved golden ring displaying an eagle, the ring he was given when he was adopted by a Nisga'a family. Like Newman and McGeer,

Bauer remains fascinated by orcas and by finding ways to protect them. "What we are terrestrially, they are in the aquatic world."

Despite his reticence to share his story publicly, Bauer is proud of his role in Operation Killer Whale. "Had we not saved the whale instead of killing it, we might still be in the dark and fail to understand and appreciate them. It was an important step to understanding that they are highly intelligent creatures, not killers."

Months later, I was writing this on Saturna Island, waiting to see Moby's family for myself, feeling like I was doing too good a job of reliving the original whale hunt. The whales were nowhere to be found. I was visiting the Fog Alarm Building to see if their local history displays sparked any ideas for this book, when one of the volunteers showed me an email they'd received that morning. "Hi, my family lived at East Point lightstation in the early 1960s, as my father, Pete Fletcher was assistant light keeper. My dad has passed away, but my mother, June Fletcher, is still alive and remembers the Moby Doll period very well."

June Fletcher was taking her daughter back to the island for their first visit since the 1970s. We met at the Fog Alarm Building, and after sharing stories of life on Saturna, June offered to show me where Burich and Bauer had camped, the spot where she had collected water samples, and where the whale hunters had mounted their harpoon. After leading me down the hill, and joking that there must have been fewer steps fifty years earlier, since she'd regularly made the walk with two young children in tow, Fletcher held her photos of Burich and Bauer's etchings next to the faded lines they'd carved into the sandstone. As she reminisced about how she used to watch for the whales, a dozen orcas from K pod surfaced off East Point as if saying hello to an old friend.

I thought about how the whales seemed to know about the machine gun on Vancouver Island and the harpoon on Sparrow's boat and later on East Point, how Moby showed up just after the hunt was called off, and now, here they were for June. Like so many of the orca experts I've met, I was convinced these beings have an intuition beyond our understanding.

I watched the whales swim free in the Salish Sea, and I watched one of the first people to catalog their habits laugh at the sight. Beautiful. Wild. Alien. And I was reminded why people like Watson, Balcomb, Ford, and Spong devote their lives to saving the whales and why people like Bauer, Burich, McGeer, and Newman were willing to risk their lives to understand them.

ACKNOWLEDGMENTS

SINCE I FIRST started sharing my obsession with this great black-and-white whale, so many amazing people have helped me tell the story—in my documentary, on CBC radio series *Ideas*, in the *Walrus*, and, of course, in this book, which I first dreamed of writing in 1996.

First off, I have to thank Joe Bauer, Pat McGeer, June Fletcher, Chris Angus, Terry McLeod, Kathy Newman, and Murray Newman for trusting me with their astonishing whale tale. And I owe a serious salute to Captain Paul Watson for introducing me to this story and, of course, for everything he's done for the world of whales.

The first person on board my own private *Pequod* was my friend Joan Watterson, who charmed Murray Newman during that initial interview, provided me with research material that was invaluable in preparing this book, and was the first reader for early drafts of every chapter.

Since then, there have been so many people who've tried to help me bring this story to life on-screen or in print, including Andrea Moodie, Barry Stevens, Michael Chechik, Lawrie Rotenberg, and Jon Cooksey. Thanks to Kyle Bornais, Farpoint Films, and Middle Child Films for funding my trip to Saturna for the conference and, especially, Middle Child's president Tony Wosk for his passionate efforts on behalf of this project in every incarnation at every stage of development. Also, thanks to Darron Leiren-Young, Matthew Chipera, Bob Hogg, Heather Wolfe, Donna Wong-Juliani, Ian Ferguson, Wray Arenz, and Art Norris, for their support in sharing this story.

Richard Blagborne and the Saturna Island Heritage Committee helped make this book possible by reminding Murray Newman that his story mattered. Among the people who helped me out on Saturna—Jude White, who wrangled interviews and photos; Athena George; Senator Pat Carney; Nancy Angermeyer; Maureen Welton; Larry Peck; Silas Stilchuck, Travis Stolting; and the Reverend David Wylie, who loaned me his home on Saturna to work on this book.

I also received some heroic assistance from part-time Saturna resident Charles Campbell, who loves Moby's story as much as I do. A brilliant writer and an even better editor, Charles was my boss, champion, and mentor when I was starting my career as a journalist at the *Georgia Straight*. Because the world is impossibly small, Charles was also my Saturna Sherpa, introducing me to everyone because he practically grew up on the island and is a cousin of Pat McGeer. He also provided invaluable advice as I explored this story. I also want to thank all the people of Saturna for doing so much to look after Moby's clan.

I'll also be eternally grateful to the orca experts who welcomed me to their pod and have been so generous with their time and wisdom, including John Ford, Kenneth Balcomb, Lance Barrett-Lennard, Howard Garrett, Paul Spong, Kristen Kanes, Jason Colby, Peter Ross, and Scott Renyard. These people didn't just agree to be interviewed— they answered my questions throughout my attempts at telling this story and walked me through the science and history. Orca expert Erich Hoyt hasn't just been an invaluable resource; when he read the original title, *The Killer Whale that Changed the World*, he politely urged me to see if my publisher would change "that" to "who."

Thanks to all the other people who've been willing to answer my questions, including Rex Weyler; Graeme Ellis; Briony Penn; Patrick Helbling from the Marineland of the Pacific Historical Society; Gulf Island historian Patrick Brown; Ann Dreolini and Deana Lancaster from the Vancouver Aquarium Marine Science Centre; Michael P. Dyer, senior maritime historian at the New Bedford Whaling Museum; Daniel Francis; Charlotte Epstein; Lori Marino; Caitlin Birdsall; Dag Ingemar Børrensen, managing director of the

Whaling Museum in Sandefjord, Norway; Scott Wallace from the David Suzuki Foundation; and Brett Soberg and the team at Eagle Wing Whale & Wildlife Tours (especially Valerie Shore and Clint Rivers), who made it possible for me to meet J pod and Granny. And apologies to anyone else who has helped over the last two decades whom I've accidentally overlooked.

I've had several university students assist me in telling this story, and their contributions have played a major role in ensuring that this book didn't take me another ten years to write. Thanks to Nancy Powell, Hayley Copperthwaite, Max Potter, Sara Goldie, Florence Ng, and especially Chantal Strand, Summer Goulden, Jess Edwards, and Lily Campbell. When I looked for assistance with this, I was hoping I might find someone to help me transcribe my interviews or do a bit of basic research and fact-checking. I never imagined I'd find students who were so passionate and qualified to assist in telling this story. Summer reviewed hundreds of newspapers from 1964 and unearthed many of the quirkier historical nuggets. Chantal, a master's of journalism student at UBC, approached me two years after an official stint as my co-op student, offering to help with research because she'd fallen in love with Moby. Jess was a vital early reader and a wonderfully obsessive researcher. Lily, an ocean sciences student and documentary filmmaker, spent the summer of 2014 studying whales on Saturna Island and the spring and summer of 2015 walking me through their world.

Also, thanks to Charlotte Gill and the brilliant readers from my UBC creative nonfiction class (Tanja Bartel, Wendy Bone, Mason Hanrahan, Tara Mitchell, and Colin Sterling) for their notes, questions, and suggestions, and my lawyer, Warren Sheffer, for all of his assistance. I'll also be forever grateful to the University of Victoria Writing Department for awarding me their 2015 Harvey Southam Fellowship, which helped me find the time to tell this story—and many of the students who assisted in researching it.

Thanks to Sasha Chapman, my editor at the *Walrus*, for all her help; fact-checker Max Halparin for his assistance with Moby myth-busting; and the *Walrus* for giving me my first chance to share Moby's story in print.

This book would not exist without the passion of former CBC radio producer Yvonne Gall, who fell in love with Moby and worked tirelessly to help me craft his story for radio. And thanks to *Ideas* host Paul Kennedy and everyone at CBC who helped make the show happen, including archivist extraordinaire Colin Preston. The night Yvonne and I won a Jack Webster Award for Best Radio Documentary in western Canada, Greystone publisher Rob Sanders stopped me as Yvonne and I were en route to get our photo taken with the trophy. "Congratulations," he said. "We have to do a book about this." I thanked him but thought he was kidding—until the next day when he called and invited me to meet the Greystone team. Thanks to Greystone all-stars Shirarose Wilensky for her copyediting and copy advice, managing editor Jennifer Croll and proofreader Stephen Ullstrom for keeping a sharp eye on everything, Peter Cocking for the splashy cover that took my breath away the moment I saw it, and especially my amazing editor, Nancy Flight, who has played an invaluable role in shaping this story. Thank you, Rob, Nancy, and everyone else at Greystone for helping me catch my whale.

Love and thanks to my dad, Hall Leiren, for always encouraging me to chase great stories, and my mom, Carol Leiren, for taking me to meet Skana and the other whales, for all your advice on this book, and for always being an inspiration.

And a million mahalos to my partner, Rayne Benu, who has encouraged, inspired, and fought with me to do the best work I was capable of on this book, the articles, and the documentaries, and for capturing magical footage of Granny breaching in the twilight and an awe-inspiring superpod celebration.

And, finally, thanks to Moby Doll, Granny, J pod, and all the orcas still out there. I hope sharing your story helps you keep living it.

Saturna Island, July 5, 2015

(revised Sarpsborg, Norway, June 1, 2016)

DECLARATION OF RIGHTS for Cetaceans: Whales and Dolphins
Based on the principle of the equal treatment of all persons;

Recognizing that scientific research gives us deeper insights into the complexities of cetacean minds, societies and cultures;

Noting that the progressive development of international law manifests an entitlement to life by cetaceans;

We affirm that all cetaceans as persons have the right to life, liberty and wellbeing.

We conclude that:

1. Every individual cetacean has the right to life.
2. No cetacean should be held in captivity or servitude; be subject to cruel treatment; or be removed from their natural environment.
3. All cetaceans have the right to freedom of movement and residence within their natural environment.
4. No cetacean is the property of any State, corporation, human group or individual.
5. Cetaceans have the right to the protection of their natural environment.
6. Cetaceans have the right not to be subject to the disruption of their cultures.
7. The rights, freedoms and norms set forth in this Declaration should be protected under international and domestic law.
8. Cetaceans are entitled to an international order in which these rights, freedoms and norms can be fully realized.
9. No State, corporation, human group or individual should engage in any activity that undermines these rights, freedoms and norms.

10. Nothing in this Declaration shall prevent a State from enacting stricter provisions for the protection of cetacean rights.

Agreed, 22nd May 2010, Helsinki, Finland
www.cetaceanrights.org

IN WRITING THIS book I've primarily relied on the people who met Moby and the original news reports from 1964, Vancouver Aquarium newsletters (which were usually penned by Newman), and scientific papers from the era authored by Newman, McGeer, and others. When news reports and memories contradict each other—and they often do—I've tried to rely on the earliest and/or the most consistent versions of events to triangulate the truth.

Winston Churchill's observation that "history is written by the victors" is true, but it's mostly written by the people who make the time to tell their stories. I wish there was more to include about some of the players who died long before I had the chance to write this—especially Samuel Burich. From the moment I heard this story, I've been haunted and inspired by the image of the man who harpooned "the monster," sitting by its side, playing his harmonica, so that Moby would know he had a friend.

Pat McGeer and I finally had our long overdue lunch meeting at the Vancouver Aquarium on March 31, 2016, after he told the story of Moby Doll to an audience of three hundred people at a memorial for Newman, who had died of a stroke on March 18 at the age of ninety-two. I'd met with Newman and Kathy a few months earlier and—at the time—the aquarium's original curator seemed indestructible. McGeer urged the aquarium to build a statue of Murray Newman at the entrance. If they do, I'm hoping it's based on the image of a delighted Newman hand-feeding Moby Doll.

Apologies in advance for any errors (I will post any corrections on the book's website www.mobydoll.com, through my own site at www.leiren-young.com, and on Twitter, and revise whatever I can in future editions), though I suspect that along with actual errors, I'll discover dozens of new, contradictory versions of the same stories and family legends that are now carved in stone—just like the images Burich and Bauer left in the rocks on Saturna.

Today, tourists who wander onto the site where Burich launched his harpoon see the modern petroglyphs and are convinced they've found something historic. That's how legends are born. And if you're ever on Saturna with someone who hasn't read this—and your friend squeals with delight when they discover the "ancient images"—that can always be our secret.

SELECTED REFERENCES

Epstein, Charlotte. *The Power of Words in International Relations: Birth of an Anti-Whaling Discourse*. Cambridge, MA: MIT Press, 2008.

Ford, John K.B., and Graeme M. Ellis. *Transients: Mammal-Hunting Killer Whales of B.C., Washington State, and Southeast Alaska*. Seattle: University of Washington Press, 2005.

Ford, John K.B., Graeme M. Ellis, and Kenneth C. Balcomb. *Killer Whales: The Natural History and Genealogy of Orcinus Orca in British Columbia and Washington State*. Vancouver: University of British Columbia Press, 1999.

Francis, Daniel, and Gil Hewlett. *Operation Orca: Springer, Luna and the Struggle to Save West Coast Killer Whales*. Pender Harbour, B.C.: Harbour Publishing, 2007.

Grey, Zane. *Tales of Southern Rivers*. New York: Derrydale Press, 2000.

Horwitz, Joshua. *War of the Whales: A True Story*. New York: Simon & Schuster, 2014.

Hoyt, Erich. *Marine Protected Areas for Whales, Dolphins and Porpoises: A World Handbook for Cetacean Habitat Conservation and Planning*. New York: Routledge Publishing, 2011.

———. *Orca: The Whale Called Killer*. Richmond Hill, ON: Firefly Books, 2013.

Hunter, Bob. "Greenpeace Declaration of Interdependence." *Greenpeace Chronicles* (winter 1976–77).

Kirby, David. *Death at SeaWorld: Shamu and the Dark Side of Killer Whales in Captivity*. New York: St. Martin's Press, 2012.

Neiwert, David. *Of Orcas and Men: What Killer Whales Can Teach Us*. New York: Overlook Press, 2015.

Newman, Murray. *Life in a Fishbowl: Confessions of an Aquarium Director*. Vancouver: Douglas & McIntyre, 1994.

———. *People, Fish and Whales: The Vancouver Aquarium Story*. Pender Harbour, B.C.: Harbour Publishing, 2006.

Wallace, Scott, and Brian Gisborne. *Basking Sharks: The Slaughter of B.C.'s Gentle Giants*. Vancouver: New Star Books, 2006.

Weyler, Rex. *Greenpeace: How a Group of Journalists, Ecologists, and Visionaries Changed the World*. Vancouver: Raincoast Books, 2004.

RELATED WEBSITES

Be Whale Wise. bewhalewise.org.

Center for Whale Research. whaleresearch.com.

David Suzuki Foundation. davidsuzuki.org.

Department of Fisheries and Oceans (Canada). dfo-mpo.gc.ca.

Eden Killer Whale Museum. killerwhalemuseum.com.au.

Greenpeace. greenpeace.org.

Kimmela Center for Animal Advocacy. kimmela.org.

National Oceanic and Atmospheric Administration. nmfs.noaa.gov.

Nonhuman Rights Project. nonhumanrightsproject.org.

Orca Network. orcanetwork.org.

Russian Orcas Homepage. russianorca.com.

Salish Sea Hydrophone Network. orcasound.net.

Saturna Heritage Centre. saturnaheritage.ca.

Save Our Wild Salmon. wildsalmon.org.

Sea Shepherd Conservation Society. seashepherd.org.

The Whale Trail. thewhaletrail.org.

Vancouver Aquarium. vanaqua.org.

WDC, Whale and Dolphin Conservation. us.whales.org.

Whale Museum (Friday Harbor). whalemuseum.org.

Wild Whales B.C. Cetacean Sightings Network. wildwhales.org.

DAVID
  SUZUKI
INSTITUTE

THE DAVID SUZUKI Institute is a nonprofit organization founded in 2010 to stimulate debate and action on environmental issues. The institute and the David Suzuki Foundation both work to advance awareness of environmental issues important to all Canadians.

We invite you to support the activities of the institute. For more information please contact us at:

David Suzuki Institute
219–2211 West 4th Avenue
Vancouver, BC, Canada V6K 4S2
info@davidsuzukiinstitute.org
604-742-2899
www.davidsuzukiinstitute.org

Checks can be made payable to the David Suzuki Institute.